T0212051

Human–Computer Interaction Series

SpringerBriefs in Human-Computer Interaction

Series editors

Desney Tan, Microsoft Research, USA
Jean Vanderdonckt, Université catholique de Louvain, Belgium

More information about this series at http://www.springer.com/series/15580

Adrian David Cheok

Hyperconnectivity

 Springer

Adrian David Cheok
Imagineering Institute
Iskandar
Malaysia

and

Department of Computer Science
City, University of London
London
UK

ISSN 1571-5035
Human–Computer Interaction Series
ISBN 978-1-4471-7309-0   ISBN 978-1-4471-7311-3   (eBook)
DOI 10.1007/978-1-4471-7311-3

Library of Congress Control Number: 2016960028

Printed on acid-free paper

This Springer imprint is published by Springer Nature
The registered company is Springer-Verlag London Ltd.
The registered company address is: 236 Gray's Inn Road, London WC1X 8HB, United Kingdom

Adrian David Cheok dedicates this book to his Grandmother Anna Pantahos (February 4th 1933 to 12th September 2015):

Dear Γιαγιά, you were the greatest, kindest, sweetest, and most loving Grandmother. I'm eternally thankful for your endless love and caring. May you always rest in peace in Heaven.

Chamari Edirisinghe dedicates this book to her Parents:

To my parents, who passed away recently: you will forever be somewhere in my heart always with love and gratitude.

Dedication Photo: (from top to bottom, left to right, first appearance): 1) Anna Pantahos, 2) Kotoko Cheok, 3) Emmanuel Pantahos, 4) Adrian David Cheok.

Prologue

In the town there were two mutes, and they were always together (McCuller C, 1940,
The Heart is a Lonely Hunter)

At the moment of birth, driven by instinct, the baby creates a bond with the person who brought it into the world. The vitality of life obliges it to do so. A baby is programmed to receive and give signals, and more importantly, depends on them to survive.

The way it can connect with other members of its species and with the world it belongs to determine the success of its vital mission. It is part of a species who possesses the extraordinary ability to develop infinite connections. It is equipped with one of the most spectacular sensorial systems in the universe. Furthermore, its ancestors were capable of designing codes and languages that has brought its capacity of connecting to an unimaginable extent. Today, it tries to pass on this ability to all bodies on earth, living and inanimate as if they were afraid of being excluded from this binding circuit. It feels the need to avoid it. It continuously creates links to be able to connect everything almost pervasively. This is how the human being, a living representation of matter, has decided to share energy.

Could one, however, find a way to conserve its capacity to be moved by sharing a glance with another…?

Mugaritz, Spain   Chef Andoni Luis Aduriz

Preface

I deeply thank my Research Fellows as well as Ph.D. students Chamari Edirisinghe, Kasun Karunanayake, and Emma Yann Zhang as well as Dr. David Levy, without whose help this book would not be possible.

I also deeply thank Chef Andoni Luis Aduriz for writing an excellent and visionary prologue and Hernán Ortiz for writing an awesome and futuristic Epilogue.

Ironically, this book about hyperconnectivity took several years longer to finish than expected, because of the seemingly never-ending overload of work in our always on $24 \times 7 = 168$ hyperconnected world. I thank Springer for their patience and support, especially from the Editorial Director of Computer Science, the amazing Beverley Ford.

My thanks to colleagues, mentors, collaborators, and friends Prof. Hiroshi Ishiguro, Prof. Masahiko Inami, Prof. Ichiya Nakamura for their help, advice, support, and friendship. Thank you to colleagues supporting and encouraging my work at City, University of London, especially Dr. Lyn Robinson and Prof. Ken Grattan. Thank you to my Ph.D. supervisor Assoc. Prof. Nesimi Ertugrul, who is always my great mentor and advisor, as well as kind friend. Thank you to the hard working staff and students at my lab in Malaysia, Imagineering Institute.

I would like to thank my Grandfather, Emmanuel Pantahos, my grandmother Anna Pantahos is heaven, and my Mother, Frida Cheok, for their love, inspiration, life advice, and support. Thank you to my daughter Kotoko for all her wonderful love and bringing me so much happiness and joy.

Iskandar, Malaysia

Adrian David Cheok

Contents

List of Figures

List of Tables

Chapter 1
Introduction

Abstract In this chapter, we introduce the historical aspects of communication media which relate to the modern phenomena of hyperconnectivity. Hyperconnectivity is a result of many interlinking historical developments in media, engineering, and computer science. We discuss the means and needs of communication among humans in the modern era. We then describe in detail the applications, potential effects on society of hyperconnectivity. Finally, we project into the future of our hyperconnected world.

Keywords Communication · Connectivity · Internet

1.1 History of Communication and Technological Advances

1.1.1 From Nonverbal to Digital

As we walk down a street, we make eye contacts with strangers, smile or greet acquaintances, and stop to talk to friends, while looking at our surrounding, and having an internal monologue with ourselves about the environment, and people we talk to. All through this time, we may text message a friend in another city about things we saw or talked about, and browse the web for more information about something that caught our attention. We may keep up with the office communication through emails, and we could be uploading a few images of what we deemed as of interest onto our social media for our friends, from all over the world, to see. It appears to be that we are constantly communicating throughout our day: nonverbally, verbally, textually, digitally, externally, internally, and globally. Our communications are part of our everyday life, and with the added advantage of technology, our communications are rapid, global, and highly technology-aided.

Communication is a very old practice. It began with the need of humans to express their messages effectively. The necessity for effective communication is a result of the expanded parameters of communication, for example, the need to

© The Author(s) 2016
A.D. Cheok, *Hyperconnectivity*, SpringerBriefs in Human–Computer Interaction,
DOI 10.1007/978-1-4471-7311-3_1

develop the hand gestures and verbal noises to include more expressions. When prehistoric communities increased in population, their communications became multifaceted with complexities of interrelationships and thoughts. The limitations in gesturing and verbal noises hindered the power relationships, since effective communication is imperative to building and maintaining societal power. Thus, the necessity for communicating messages effectively is driven by the need to build productive relations and control interrelations (Poe 2010).

Language, a system of communication for expression and interpretation, which was an integral part of the human evolution, was a very significant development in the history of communication. From gesturing and verbal shouts, humans developed a set of words that are commonly understood, interpreted, and utilized, which is a milestone in human communication. Language was used verbally before it turned into characters used for writing.

Talking came naturally to people. The verbal noises of yesterdays turned into verbal set of words that were commonly understood as conveying certain meanings. According to Poe (2010), talking or the verbal use of language developed because it was an evolutionary advantage to talk. The cognitive ability to talk and understand a set of words and the capacity to talk has advanced simultaneously. For more than 150,000 years, people talked and developed a set of social and moral values, and built early economic base and fundamentals on authority. Since a human is biologically formed with eyes, ears, and a mouth, with a cognitive capacity to understand and interact, talking is an easy task. Poe (2010) argues the ability to talk, listen, and understand created a certain egalitarian environs, in terms of communication. It could have been possible because of the size of the community was small. However, the power balance most possibly has been in favor of the individuals who have shown considerable skills at talking. On the other hand, talking is sharing knowledge, making the community smart for the common good, such as shared knowledge combined with shared skills, made hunting and gathering productive.

Nonverbal and verbal communication has developed naturally, without being invented. Written language has been the first invention in communication. With language, it became possible to communicate any message, even the most complex messages, within a limited space. Written language shifted the method of communication, even though it created a division among the society. The powers behind the written language were commonly rulers and religious leaders, which provided them with a special dominance over others. Written language developed with the means to communicate, first with clay tablets, papyrus, and stone, and each improved the characters and articulation of written language. This changes the communication pattern and builds a hierarchy within the process of communication, dividing individuals into three sets: the language savvy, those who associated with language savvy, and those who do not know the language.

It has always been assumed until much later that to the communication, it is required to hasten the messenger, because the efficacy of the message is in the fast delivery. Instead of concentrating on the means of communication, in those days, people concentrated on speeding up the messenger, thus the excellent road system of Persians and Romans, and fast horses. However, the point of reference here is the attention paid to speeding the communication, achieved through improving the infrastructure.

The printing revolutionized the communication, by providing the opportunities to communicate to many. This also to a certain degree democratized the learning and education, changing the perception of the information and communication. Printing was the first approach toward information availability, providing opportunities for expanding the reach of communication. It released the monopoly on information and learning, and created a new educated class, who became the new middle class in the society. Printing changed information accessibility and learning, changed the social order, toppled regimes, and toppled the religious order of Europe, leading to the renaissance.

A few centuries later, television achieved a similar kind of change which McLuhan saw as a 'global village phenomenon' (McLuhan 1994). Television created audio/visual contents, bringing it to the sitting rooms of homes, thus breaking the association of information with place and bringing multisensory experience. Internet has destroyed the obstacles associated with place, speed, and information accessibility. First with personal computers, and broadband, and later with mobile phones, Internet created a society that is highly dependent on high-speed accessibility to information. Nowadays, the mere connectivity between individuals has turned a new page toward hyperconnectivity, where everything (human, non-human, and objects) can all be connected through embedded technologies. Hyperconnectivity will bring a new era of communication, changing the means of communication, and individual perception of the need to communicate.

1.2 Modern Communication

1.2.1 Means of Communicating and the Need to Communicate

Societies have been shaped more by the nature of the media by which men communicate than by the content of the communication

Quoting Lister (2009, p. 89), this was said by MacLuhan in 1964, highlighting the importance of the role of media in our society. He suggested that electronic media, from telegraph to computers, are reshaping our interactions that the media is becoming an extension of man. In the print media era, the experience of media communication is a sequential process, limited to a particular system, whereas the contemporary experience of communication is numerous, synchronized, and often multisensory. Individual experience of media communication is multifaceted with our media communications being simultaneously audio, visual, verbal, and textual. Our means of communication has influenced our need to communicate.

Throughout our history, when prehistoric humans painted their experiences to the creation of language, our need to communicate far exceeded the means. When the Paleolithic humans painted the caves in Altamira, Spain, and Lascaux, France, they were trying to communicate their visual experiences through art, creating a visual picture. The need to share and preserve the experience drove the Paleolithic men and women of those caves to find a means of communication. That became the first means of communication which was driven by the desire to communicate. The verbal form of communication is once again the development, due to the limitations in the nonverbal communication, thus a need that shaped the method. The population growth had encouraged the early humans to create a form of control; thus, the need to communicate verbally became a highest requirement.

At this point in history, the means of communication became the controlling power of the need to communicate, because few became creators of vocabulary. Oratory ability and the ability to articulate has seen the shift from the need to communicate, and the means of communication, because the means of communication was under the control of a group who has the ability to generate and manage the language. Yet, there are times in history that the means and the need went hand in hand to create communications, such as the era of great Greek philosophers that is celebrated even to this day. The written language created a division between the individuals who can write and who cannot, thus giving a new interpretation to the inclusion. The written language controlled the need to communicate by limiting the access to the means of communication.

The arrival of print media revolutionized the communication by giving it a mobility that is not fixed to a place. Though there still exists the problem of inclusion, print media changed the shape of the accessibility to information. With the accessibility, the means of communication became approachable, to change the need to communicate. Education and learning became approachable, with far-reaching consequences in the relationship between means of communication and need to communicate. As McLuhan argued, it was the audio/visual media that made the means of communication transform the need to communicate.

Contemporary media communication has moved forward, far ahead than McLuhan has envisioned. Our means of communication has completely taken over our association with the need to communicate. Our need to communicate, as mentioned before, has been developing from the time of evolution. Today, the technological and communication advancement has changed the perception of need to communicate, making the need a necessity that is government by the means of communication. The new media environs envelop us, making our everyday an experience of participation. McLuhan has envisioned the new communication media transforming the world into a "global village," where every corner of the earth is connected through information sharing. He has written that any remote corner on earth with a television is as cosmopolitan as any big city (McLuhan 1969). Today, any corner on earth is as cosmopolitan as any city through the connectivity and availability of information. New research and experiments in pervasive computing are making it possible for the world to become hyperconnected, where everything that can communicate and will communicate at all times.

1.3 What Is Hyperconnectivity?

Over the past few decades, there has been a revolution in computing and communication. Machines that once occupied whole rooms have moved to the desktop,
the lap, hand, even into clothing, and inside the human body itself. The Internet has
shifted from connecting computers to connecting objects all around us. We have
now entered the era of the Internet of things and pervasive computing (Cheok
2015). We, as humans, can now extend our senses and brains into the world. New
technologies allow us to facilitate these new communications and to create natural
and humanistic ways of interfacing with machines, as well as other people remotely
over large distances using the full range of human gestures such as touch, sight,
sound, and even taste and smell.

Hyperconnectivity is a relatively new word that was invented to describe this
rapid availability and very broad and global assimilation of entirely new ways to
communicate through digital networks (Dutta and Bilbao-Osorio 2012).
Hyperconnectivity is not merely the technology that facilitates communication but
also the impact this technology has at both local and global level, on everyday lives,
finances, governance, and social interactions. Hyperconnectivity results from a
combination of wider availability of broadband Internet expansion, the exponential
growth in proliferation of mobile and wearable computing devices, and high-speed
wireless Internet access. It includes the dominance of social media and
consumer-generated media in daily life and the use of the cloud for data and
application access.

Fredette et al. (2012) had noted hyperconnectivity possesses certain key characteristics. It is status of "always on" because broadband and mobile devices keep
individuals connected 24/7 globally without borders. The accessibility is becoming
increasingly uncomplicated and easy due to the growing smartness of mobile
devices and interconnections between mobile devices and personal computers. The
other factor is the richness of available information, which has extrapolated to a
degree that it has reached the point of overload, and yet the availability of information whether local or global or inconsequential or deliberate plays a major role in
changing the results of connectivity. Hyperconnectivity is interactive, everything is
connected to just about everything, and so is everyone. This is not just about people
and connecting people, but this is people-to-machine, machine-to-machine, and
machine-to-people-to-machine connections, which is also termed as the Internet of
things. The final aspect is that all communications are semi-permanently recorded,
through various apparatus and sensors and also because individuals are in the habit
of limitlessly recording their everyday activities.

Hyperconnectivity has the potential to overcome the limitations of time and
space. It has separated us from our association with place, making us universal in our
experiences because we are no longer required to be at one place to communicate.
Recently, the world has become increasingly hyperconnected. We now live in an
environment where the Internet and its digital media and apps are readily accessible
and immediate, where humans can communicate with each other instantly, and

where machines are equally interconnected through sensors and actuators connected with each other through the Internet. Hyperconnectivity is revolutionizing the perception of individual relationships, consumer relations, and citizen engagement. As a result, there will be fundamental changes in our economical practices, societal norms, ethics and morals, and our political practices and engagement. For the first time in human history, hyperconnectivity will make it possible to bring people (and machines and objects and things) together from anywhere and anytime. Its impact is both ubiquitous and pervasive and nonstop. Hyperconnectivity has also given rise to a globalized "168" world (24 × 7 = 168), where the work and play day continues around the clock, the pulse of society and business never ceasing.

Hyperconnectivity and pervasive computing will bring about radical developments in every aspect of human lives in the form of new kinds of symbioses between humans and computers; it will drive a revolution in finance, communications, manufacturing, business, government administration, societal infrastructure, entertainment, training, and education.

1.3.1 Applications of Hyperconnectivity in Society

Presently, most human interactions with computers are conducted via input devices such as the keyboard and screen. However, in the future, the computer will be embedded in almost every object in our environment and be an integral part of almost all of our work, learning, and play. Internet media and pervasive computing refer to the natural and humanistic ways that humans interface with the digital gadgets and devices as well as with other people through the Internet using the full range of human gestures and senses. Soon our entire environment will become a distributed computer and respond almost like human to people's needs and actions in a contextual manner. Interaction with the Internet and digital world will be embodied in the physical environment, rather than on a computer system. Humans as physical beings now actually become surrounded by digital media.

Through hyperconnected pervasive computing and creative Internet media, new computer and cybernetic systems that will improve our lives and create new and seemingly remarkable possibilities in human society will develop. We can foresee a future where, instead of humans needing to adapt themselves to computers and electronic systems, computers interact with people in a totally natural and human-like manner to make life easier. Some samples of the hyperconnectivity and creative Internet media include the following:

Mixed Reality—where computer-generated objects are merged with the real world. A person in mixed reality environment is able to see and interact with both real world and virtual objects. This will extend to all of the senses including audio–visual, touch, taste, and smell.

Internet of Things—everyday objects connected continuously to networks and are readable, recognizable, locatable, addressable, and/or controllable via the Internet. Everyday objects include not only the electronic devices we encounter

Table 1.1 Examples of some future products that will use hyperconnected computing technologies

Multisensory communication	3D collaborative environment	Mixed reality games	Future learning
People around the world can communicate all their senses and experiences through the Internet, including touches, tastes, and smells, with sensing and actuation in all their personal and external environments	Users interacting in 3D environment on the same project. Users can be sited at different locations around the world in true 3D collaboration for work or learning	New form of entertainment that combines physical and virtual world interactions, mobility, and ubiquitous computing	New forms of collaborative learning where through new electronic books and media and pervasive computing, learning is done by experience and doing

every day, but things that we do not ordinarily think of as electronic at all such as food, clothing, materials, commodities, landmarks; and all the miscellany of commerce and culture.

Internet Classroom—in the twenty-first century, all knowledge transfer can be done through the Internet, and classrooms and universities will be transformed into creative workshops where learning is through collaborative and connected learning by doing. Table 1.1 shows some examples of products where these technologies can be used.

Hyperconnected computing technologies have many current and future applications in almost all industrial and lifestyle fields where humans and the environment will be connected to Internet and communicating with all senses. These applications include learning, healthcare, games, entertainment, transport, building and architecture, manufacturing, and environment.

1.3.2 Promises of Hyperconnectivity

Hyperconnectivity will create new prospects for human-to-machine, machine-to-machine, and machine-to-human-to-machine interactions. New studies in ubiquitous computing, with sensors and actuations, embedded into everyday apparatus could make life easier for individuals with special needs, or make urban living a quality experience by experimenting on infrastructure. Studies on digital multisensory experiences contribute to generating sensory feelings digitally and present new avenues of study. New studies in robotics are contributing tremendously to improvements in human–machine relationships.

We will discuss several concepts in the next few chapters to highlight the possibilities offered by new connectedness. In the second chapter, we will explore the Poetry Mix-up, a project developed with the intention of promoting values of distinctive cultures, which will help in improving social relations. This project is a platform to communicate literature, especially poetry through digital media. This is an example of interactions between humans and machines, for entertainment, for learning, and for cultural sharing.

In Chap. 3, we will introduce electrical, magnetic, and thermal interfaces that can create and modify taste and smell sensations with new interactions. The chapter will propose an idea of digital olfaction and gustation as input and output for interaction for creating and experiencing digital representation of food. It will allow multisensory Internet communication including taste and smell in the hyperconnected future.

In Chap. 4, we will discuss a controversial topic of intimacy with robots. We will explore several deliberations the subject of love and sex with robots, which was first discussed by Levy (2007), and will present some projects on robotics and intimate relations. In the hyperconnected future, robots will play a major role in various fields and most notably in reinterpreting our relationship with machines, especially regarding humanoid robots. It is crucial to build a dialogue on the moral and ethical philosophies of the appropriation of robots as human companions.

In the fifth chapter, we will explore the several aspects of the impact of hyperconnectivity on everyday practices and long-term policy and planning. We will conclude this book by emphasising the sustainability of hyperconnectivity.

1.3.3 Future of Hyperconnectivity

Hyperconnectivity is everything communicating by any means, from one to one, from one to many, and many to one. An unimaginable amount of data is transferring and being stored, which makes data the new currency of the future of hyperconnectivity (Biggs et al. 2012). The rapid growth of data traffic has created a problem of containing and providing greater service, to which telecommunication operator service providers have answered with restrictions on usage by traffic throttling, filtering, and use of data threshold. This practice has been questioned and discussed at great length, leading to the debate over "net neutrality" (Biggs et al. 2012). However, there have been efforts to accommodate the uncontrollable growth of data by investing in networks and infrastructure, and improving capacity and speed.

Hyperconnectivity is promising to be the everyday experience of our lives. It will rearrange the boundaries that exist in our lives, making them blur with far reaching outcomes. Many industries, such as energy, transport, healthcare, and finance, are relying on hyperconnected solutions to manage, monitor, and deliver their services. There are certain risks associated with the hyperconnected environs, since every aspect is connected. This breadth of connectedness leads to highly connected information environment, where the greatest threat is information hacking, by which certain information can unintentionally be handed to individuals who should not have access (Biggs et al. 2012). These risks should not impede the development of hyperconnected environs, considering the opportunities it offers. However, these opportunities and risks will determine the limitations of accessibility, in terms of determining who and what in granting the accession. This will also determine the role of the regulator and the negative and positive consequences of regulating. The telecommunication/ICT regulator's role will encompass a wide variety of responsibilities to face challenges of a hyperconnected world.

Hyperconnectivity will encourage to both increase and limit who has access to information. The information will have a high significance in the digital world, with information creation, and skills using digital tools are considered as an advantage. Individuals with poor digital literacy will face the problems of inclusion in certain key areas, being unable to move ahead. The future of connected world will be of information: who can access, share, and profit from information.

Expansions in online education in the hyperconnected society will change the perception of learning and education. Higher educational Institutions like the Massachusetts Institute of Technology have freed their course work material making them accessible to anyone willing to study. An example success story is Ahaan Rungta who studies through the OpenCourseWare program of MIT from the age of 5 and succeeded in entering the undergraduate level of MIT by the age of 15 (Everett 2015). The future education will be focusing on recognizing the informal education, and the merits of unconventional education which will empower individuals for the challenge of hyperconnectivity.

Political engagement will experience a change within the hyperconnectivity, with individuals engaging through digital media. It will no longer be a local participatory politics but global in outreach with the understanding that connectedness brings new political realities. Information availability will empower individuals, demand transparency and accountability from governing institutions in the quest for smarter governing.

Hyperconnected future will build networks of people and things that will build unimaginable global connections. It is an embedded, pervasive, and invisible network that will be visible only through interactions, and it holds vast amount of data moving constantly. The challenges of hyperconnected world will be numerous that can be faced by developing strong yet flexible policies and best practices.

References

Biggs P, Johnson T, Lozanova Y, Sundberg N (2012) Emerging issues for our hyperconnected world. The global information technology report, pp 47–56

Cheok AD (ed) (2015) Introduction to hyperconnectivity. Lambert Academic Publishing

Dutta S, Bilbao-Osorio B (2012) The global information technology report 2012: living in a hyperconnected world

Everett L (2015) Homeschooled with MIT courses at 5, accepted to MIT at 15. MIT News. Retrieved 18 Apr 2016, from http://news.mit.edu/2015/ahaan-rungta-mit-opencourseware-mitx-1116

Fredette J, Marom R, Steiner K, Witters L (2012) The promise and peril of hyperconnectivity for
    organizations and societies. The global information technology report, pp 113–119
Levy D (2007) Love + sex with robots. HarperCollins, New York
Lister M (2009) New media: a critical introduction. Taylor & Francis
McLuhan M (1969) Counterblast
McLuhan M (1994) Understanding media: the extensions of man. MIT press
Poe MT (2010) A history of communications: media and society from the evolution of speech to
    the internet. Cambridge University Press

Chapter 2
Modeling Literary Culture Through Interactive Digital Media

Abstract In the rapidly transforming landscape of the modern world, people unconsciously refrain from interacting in public spaces, containing their communications that are extensive and universal within the home and relatively individually. The mass connectivity and technological advancement created new cultural values, thus altering the human perception of the world. This state of affairs is jeopardizing some of the cultural identities that have surmounted few centuries, shaping the values and associated customs of numerous generations. Furthermore, computer technology became integrated exceedingly with the modern culture, which prompted us to introduce and explore the avenues of cultural computing that is the familiar ground of the modern society. With the intention of promoting values of distinct cultures, which will greatly assist in enhancing social relationships, we have developed a framework to communicate literature through digital media, which introduced the platform to create Poetry Mix-up.

Keywords Cultural computing · Poetry · Social connectivity

2.1 Introduction

The word "*culture*" was originated from Latin word "*cultura*" meaning "to cultivate," which began to appear in the English language during the late eighteenth century. The intellectual and spiritual cultivation of an individual or a societal group was the notion of culture during the late eighteenth century. Culture has been defined in multitude of ways by the scholars of various disciplines. Williams (2001) in "The Analysis of Culture" defined culture in three categories: first, the "ideal" in which culture is the state or the process of human perfection: second, the "documentary" that refers to the body of intellectual and imaginative work being deemed as culture; and third, the "social" in which culture is a description of a certain way of life, which expresses its meanings and values in art, learning, institutions, and behavioral patterns. To Geertz (1973), culture is semiotic. He described man as an animal suspended in a web of significance, which Geertz understands as culture,

© The Author(s) 2016

A.D. Cheok, *Hyperconnectivity*, SpringerBriefs in Human–Computer Interaction, DOI 10.1007/978-1-4471-7311-3_2 and the study of culture as an interpretative one in search of meanings. Hannerz (1992) believed that culture is collective and above all a matter of meanings. He further added that culture is the meaning that people create and which creates people as members of society.

In the contemporary society, the meanings and values are communicated in great speed and in a variety of ways, changing the nature of their social behaviors and interactions. According to Bakardjieva (2003), who wrote about virtual togetherness, communal interactions were transformed to the socialization of private experience through a new form of social organization. For instance, in Facebook or Twitter, new forms of social communities are created, linking people of different backgrounds, demographics, etc., allowing the flow of personal experiences.

Communicating the established cultural aspects, which will provide the contemporary society with common communication grounds and familiar grounds for "reaching out," has to be cultivated within the same environment utilizing the existing channels, thus influencing the participation. The approachability and accessibility to interact with cultural elements will be the key factors with the users. Moreover, the integration of "cultural layer" and "computer layer" introduces intense challenges (Manovich 2001). Thus, computer technology has moved beyond the realm of being a tool, transforming and creating the definition of the modern society.

Cultural computing uses various methods to model established cultures so that users could interact and experience these cultures through modern computing applications. As creativity is the mutual foundation of culture, science, and technology, cultural computing explores and develops technology to advance creative activities that would be a positive impact on contemporary lifestyles. On the other hand, this is an example of interactions between humans and machines, for the purpose of entertainment, learning, and cultural sharing. In this article, we present an outline of the cultural computing research and the main features of cultural computing. We then present our cultural computing prototype: Poetry Mix-up.

2.2 Background

The need to establish a computer technology that increases the communal communications and cultural exchange has always been a zealous research concern. There have been various efforts in the field of computing to restore the rapidly decaying cultural aspects, thus promoting social communication using new dimensions or mediums to explore culture. The purpose behind this technology is not only to reconnect and strengthen human relationships, but also to encourage in accepting and welcoming diverse nature of global cultures.

Connectivity is the pulse of culture. Information flowed through connectivity in the form of symbols and values. Williams (2001) believed that symbols and values that he described as patterns are the key to understanding culture. The encoding and decoding of cultural codes in this communication process depend on the connectivity of greater strength. One scream from a female is culturally encoded and decoded, allocating values and meanings to the action. In turn begins the process of the acceptance and rejection of each nuance that would develop through several centuries and pass on to several generations. This interpersonal connectivity, which shaped meanings and values attached to each action for centuries, has been transformed to mass connectivity, which initiates universal values and meanings. Manuel Castells (Amoore 2005) described this as the material arrangement that provides for social interconnections without territorial practices. He called this "the space of flows." Unfolding further, Castells argued that the present-day world is made up of the interactive and interacted, which build personal connectivity, horizontal communication that scales the territorial boundaries, creating networks of solidarity and cooperation, and social movements that heed no terrain.

Within this mass connectivity, computer technology has achieved the prominence of having no boundaries. The mass connectivity, where the cultural identities are built and affirmed, where computer technology is empowered, is the modern generator of values and meanings. This is where our question arises, whether the computer technology is a culture, or whether it serves as a medium or a tool for the cultures to develop. Pacey (1983) argued that technology is culturally neutral and that it contributes tools independent of the cultural value system and impartially support a cultural structure. In this sense, computers are technical tools that contribute to society detachedly and have no values or meanings attached. Then again, in the contemporary society, computers are a prominent part of the everyday activities, and they have created activities that are transforming the definition of time and space. Disabusing his own argument, Pacey (1983) added if technology is to be feasible, it has to correspond with the patterns of activities, which are incorporated in a distinct culture. When computer technology becomes the pattern of any culture, and it has become nowadays, it transforms the values and meanings associated with the culture, creating a culture that is associated unwaveringly to the technology. Nowadays, mobile devices have become smaller and intensely richer in features, making them "extra mobile" and highly efficient, thus creating a culture that is tremendously connected to computer technology to sustain the cultural meanings and values.

Mass connectivity and technological culture are creating new cultural values and altering our perception of the world, which is mass consumption and mass consumerization related. If we take the iPhone as an example, it is simply not just a phone of high technology but as a status symbol that symbolizes the values, perceptions, and being part of a cultural entity that is consisted of mass connectivity and technology.

This is where we suggest the unification of culture with computer technology to form cultural computing. The mass connectivity and technological culture is critically endangering the various cultural identities that are finding hard to sustain within the rapidly changing cultural environment, where the mass production of global values and meanings are being acknowledged as the acceptable. Furthermore, the modern generation is distancing themselves from the cultural values that have passed through centuries and generations, thus disengaging the related social associations.

Our intention is to introduce distinctive cultural identities, associated cultural values, and to promote social interconnectivity through an interactive computer technological process. Since this endeavor is grounded on the familiar territories of the modern generation, the computer technology, and mass connectivity, the promotion is to awake the sensibility to an immersive cultural experience, which is accessible to the populace. This enterprise will be cultivating closer relationships between generations since this will encourage the youths to study the literature of the bygone eras, while the older generation would share their cultural experiences with the young. The merge of traditional poetry lines with the new communication methods and the promotion of greater and closer interaction between young and old through shared cultural experiences will be exceedingly beneficial to the society.

2.3 Related Research

Some of the related research in cultural computing, such as ZENetic Computer (Tosa et al. 2004), provide an understanding of certain cultural values and associated meanings. ZENetic Computer uses computing as a method for cultural translation where thoughts in Zen Buddhism are used. Furthermore, augmented reality narrative like Alice (Hu et al. 2008) leads the user through virtual and real locations, moral choices, and emotional states. Another example is Hitch-Haiku (Tosa et al. 2007), where the reproduction of traditional Haiku, a Japanese minimal poem form, by computer is developed. A random expression from a chapter of Japanese essays named "1000 Books and 1000 Nights," of which the essence is created into a Haiku and translated to English by the system. Thus, the core values of the Japanese essays would be communicated to a wing of society who is unlikely to experience the traditional Japanese literary culture.

New avenues in understanding, experiencing, and appreciating cultural heritage are also being explored using virtual reality (VR) technology. Virtual reality technology provides new interactive experience by recreating the cultural heritage content in an immersive 3D environment for the users to explore and experience the culture in real time (Song et al. 2004). In the project "Interacting with the virtually recreated Peranakans" (Song et al. 2003), the re-creation of Peranakan's[1] cultural

---

[1]Peranakan Chinese or Straits-born Chinese are the descendants of Chinese immigrants who came to the Malay archipelago including British Malaya (now Peninsular Malaysia and Singapore, where they are also referred to as Baba-Nyonya) and Dutch East Indies (now Indonesia; where they are also referred as Kiau-Seng) [4] between the fifteenth and seventeenth centuries. https://en.wikipedia.org/wiki/Peranakan.

heritage incorporating intuitive interaction techniques using VR technology is a new approach to culture communication.

On the other hand, we have explored the approaches toward the fusion of cultural elements and modern computing applications in Confucius Computer (Cheok et al. 2008). Confucius Computer is a new form of illogical cultural computing based on the Eastern paradigms of balance and harmony, which are radically different from the ancient Greek logic normally experienced in computing. It aims to facilitate cultural communication by enabling people of diverse cultural backgrounds and different generations, especially the young, to gain deeper understanding of the ancient Chinese culture using the modes of communication they are familiar with. The system uses new media to revive and model these historical philosophies and teachings into three subsystems, Confucius chat, Confucius music-painting, and Confucius food, thus enabling a wider awareness of ancient culture using the literacy of digital interactivity.

2.4 Framework of Modeling Literature

The innovative examples such as mentioned in the previous paragraphs have explored the possibilities available for sustainable new interactive platform while we specifically concentrate on exploring the concepts of cultural computing to develop a framework to communicate literature.

Teamed with our line of reasoning concerning the cultural computing, and with the recognition of the significance of communication as more than sending and receiving of messages, but "a symbolic process whereby reality is produced, maintained, repaired, or transformed" (Carey 2008), we have incorporated the important characteristics from computing, communication, and culture to develop our system—Poetry Mix-up. Our system is prepared with the framework as the basis, and we believe this framework could be applicable to any form of system that is being developed for the communication of literature.

The features of the framework are described as follows:

2.4.1 Literature Regeneration

While globalizing process encourages global cultural values, there are unique cultures all over the world whose values have scaled centuries, nurturing countless generations. These are the distinctive values, which have shaped numerous communities, their beliefs, their attitudes, and their activities. These values are the promoting factor of various interrelations, intercommunications, and associated creative practices. Ancient literature is one of the profound communication channels, specifically poetry, which has created, revived, and strengthened the values in communities. Through centuries, various social spectrums of every society created their own literature to communicate and secure social connectivity.

2.4.2 Pervasive Experience

Another important characteristic of interactive computing system is to provide pervasive experience. Culture is a "way of life" or a lived experience to most people. It is an all-encompassing experience that is acutely constrained by the limited experiences such as visiting cultural museums or reading classical literatures in libraries which confine the encounters to specific locations or spaces. Therefore, interactive cultural computing should be able to merge cultural elements seamlessly into the communal lives and be able to provide pervasive cultural experience.

2.4.3 Mass Accessibility

Mass accessibility could be declared as one of the basic elements in cultural computing. Technology should be developed to accommodate the mass accessibility since it is absolutely important that people stay linked together for the cultural relationships to flourish and expand. Cultural connectivity enables people to overcome cultural barriers, like language problem, to access different cultures and exchange their cultural values. Providing the accessibility to the mass and connecting different cultural groups will greatly enhance the collective activities of people, who are separated by different thought processes of different periods, to participate in similar cultural activities and build positive communications.

2.4.4 Social Connectivity

Social connectivity is the heart of any community since it develops, defines, and improves the communications among diverse social stratums. It enriches, cultivates, and originates standpoints of the members of societies to transform their approaches and attitudes. Social connectivity reinforces the cultural associations, enabling communities to overcome cultural barriers and communication difficulties. Technology should always empower social connectivity and enhance the methodologies for further improvements.

Based on these characteristics, we developed Poetry Mix-up and compiled the features of our system in the Table 2.1, and the system will be described in the following sections in details.

Table 2.1 Cultural computing features of Poetry Mix-up

Poetry Mix-up	
Literature regeneration	By combining modern hybrid cultural elements, mobile culture, and traditional poetry, Poetry Mix-up aims to create a new and revived form of poetry writing. By mixing up different variety of poems, the system generates new poems according to the input messages. This method provides users with the opportunity to create a version of regenerated poetry together within their own familiar environment
Pervasive experience	Mobile phone provides an ideal platform for pervasive experience. People can call or send messages no matter where they are. In the Poetry Mix-up system, users could express their own thoughts by sending a SMS to a specified telephone number. According to the message, the system will create a free style poetry, thereby providing the users with the experience of creating their own poems
Mass accessibility	The process of inputting for the Poetry Mix-up system is based on short message service that is known as a highly interactive communication platform developed especially with the aim of making it accessible to the mass. Furthermore, the displaying technique used in the system introduces another dimension of accessibility since it provides cooperative accessibility
Social connectivity	Poetry is one of the indirect communication methods in most cultures from the ancient times. The Poetry Mix-up process is based on the utilization of existing poetry lines from the past. The fusion of various poem lines with the newly fed lines of thought has the effect of strengthening the understanding between different social and cultural segments in the society. It will also raise the awareness of the necessity to learn and preserve a time-honored cultural element, poetry. The system would introduce a regenerated poetic culture and would strengthen social connectivity using a modern approach

2.5 Poetry Mix-Up

2.5.1 System Overview

By blending media art and poetry, the Poetry Mix-up system was developed, and it extends existing short message service (SMS) to a new level of self-expression and public communication. Based on the user's input SMS, which is generated from his experience in the real world, the system selects few poem lines that most closely match the user's and the poets' intention, and recomposes a new poem to the user. The generated poem extends the user's reality into the virtual reality expressed in the poems, thus enabling a mixed reality experience between the user and the classical poets. This new type of mixed reality poetry experience is pervasive, as the user could instantly SMS whenever and wherever he has the motivation to do so. Therefore, the mixed reality poetry experience is closely fitted to the user context, which would welcome the user's natural appreciation. Mixing poetry is the major element of this system that transforms the users into experiencing the state of being a poet by mixing short messages into poems. It will provide a means of expression

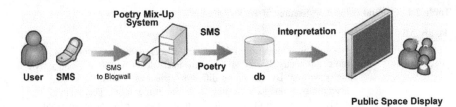

Fig. 2.1 Overview design of Poetry Mix-up

Fig. 2.2 Visualization output of Poetry Mix-up

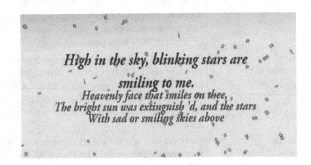

in the language that younger generation can understand and the forms of social communication, which is an essential part of their lives.

As in Fig. 2.1, the user sends a short message to the system that contains a preconfigured mobile number. Then, the extracted text from the SMS will be transferred to the processing unit, exempting any inappropriate words, be processed and mixed to generate a new poetry, and the end result will be displayed.

By providing visualization that displays messages in its natural form as shown in Fig. 2.2, the Poetry Mix-up acts as a virtual meeting point where it combines the features from literature, virtual reality, and digital communication. In the aspect of the visualization, the system provides not only good mental experience, but also intelligent and fascinating visual experience to the user.

2.5.2   Detailed System Description

In the Poetry Mix-up system, short messages are received by a dedicated GSM/GPRS modem and fetched into the system. The fetched SMS is analyzed to identify most prominent word, and a poem will be created with the means of the content. The application enables the user to assume the role of a poetry jockey. The technique used in Poetry Mix-up integrates a number of ideas from different disciplines such as information retrieval and natural language understanding, specifically word sense disambiguation (WSD) and topic summarizing, and augments the

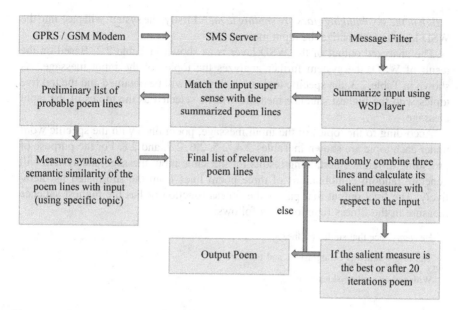

Fig. 2.3 Overview of poetry generation

system with genetic algorithm-based methods to create a model for coherent poetry output.

As shown in Fig. 2.3, after receiving the message, the system will first analyze the message using the Message Filter module in which SMS language and emoticon will be translated into normal English. The translated message will then be passed to the WSD layer for the purpose of understanding the specific meaning or sense of each word in the message. In the WSD layer, WordNet (Miller and Fellbaum 1998) is modified by adding the analysis of determiners, prepositions, pronouns, conjunctions, and particles and used as the lexical database of English words, in order to increase the accuracy of WSD. ·

The results of WSD layer will be transferred to the topic modeling layer. In this attempt, the salience measure (Boguraev and Kennedy 1999) of a particular topic is calculated, and the topics with the highest salience measure are selected. By matching the specific words and the related topics in the input message with the existing poem lines, the system will generate a preliminary list of probable poem lines in the topic summarizing layer.

In the stage of final poem mixing, 20 combinations of three poem lines will be randomly and iteratively generated from the shortlisted probable poem lines. The system will calculate the salience measure of each combination using the fitness function. The combination with highest salience measure will be output as the final poem. The unique mixing enables the system to borrow random but relative lines of poetry from different poets. Therefore, the final outcome of the system could be unusual, surprising, or maybe amusing. As an example, the user sends the SMS

"High in the sky, blinking stars are smiling to me." Firstly, the system will pass into the WSD layer to summarize the input message.

The analyzed output of the WSD layer is as shown in Table 2.2. Based on the result of WSD, the system further analyzes the topics of the input message. As shown in Table 2.3, the specific topic of each word will be obtained and the top five topics with the highest salience measure will be selected as the topics of the input message.

According to the topics of the input message, poem lines with the specific word under each topic are shown in Tables 2.4, 2.5, 2.6, 2.7, and 2.8. For the purpose of providing different entertaining results for the same input message, the system will generate random combinations of three poem lines from the shortlisted list itera- tively. The final output that passes the fitness function or has the highest salience measure in the fitness function is as follows:

> Heavenly face that smiles on thee,
>
> The bright sun was extinguish'd, and the stars
>
> With sad or smiling skies above

Table 2.9 shows more examples generated from the system.

Table 2.2 Results of the WSD layer

Word	Type	Sense
High	Adjective	Greater than normal in degree or intensity or amount
In	Preposition	A preposition
The	Connector	Singular definite connector
Sky	Noun	The atmosphere and outer space as viewed from the earth
Blinking	Adjective	(Used of persons) informal intensifiers
Star	Noun	(Astronomy) a celestial body of hot gases that radiates energy derived from thermonuclear reactions in the interior
Are	Auxiliary Verb	Have the quality of being
Smiling	Verb	A facial expression characterized by turning up the corners of the mouth; usually shows pleasure or amusement
To	Preposition	A preposition
Me	Pronoun	First person, singular, objective case, base-I

Table 2.3 Results of the topic modeling layer

Word	Category	Salience measures
Smiling	Communication	25.72
Star	Object	25.00
Sky	Substance	21.93
Are	Be	20.22
High	Attribute	16.54

Table 2.4 Shortlisted poem lines about "smiling" and "communication"

No.	Poem line
1	And, with smiles that answer their smiling
2	Heavenly face that smiles on thee
3	A smile on my face to mask the sorrow
4	Let us smile for the sake of it
5	Sweet moans, sweeter smiles

Table 2.5 Shortlisted poem lines about "star" and "object"

No.	Poem line
1	One star can guide a ship at sea
2	Till the stars shine through the roof
3	And stars for ever dwell
4	The bright sun was extinguish'd and the stars
5	Night is the mother of stars

Table 2.6 Shortlisted poem lines about "sky" and "substance"

No.	Poem line
1	The blue sky
2	Blue be the sky and soft breeze
3	Blue sky yesterday
4	Like the blue of the sky
5	But with blue sky

Table 2.7 Shortlisted poem lines about "are" and "be"

No.	Poem line
1	Their heads are bent, as if in prayerful mood
2	Life is a soul
3	At starting, is my object. Nay we'll go
4	Changing from a caterpillar was work that's true
5	The swinging spider's silver line

Table 2.8 Shortlisted poem lines about "high" and "attribute"

No.	Poem line
1	Crawling high, crawling low
2	Flitting high, flitting low
3	For he once was a star of the highest degree
4	High or low
5	A traditional music band in high spirits

Table 2.9 Three examples of input messages and output poems

Input message	Poem
I want to realize my dreams, not just record them	Records of great wishes slept with, Dream moon, cream moon, first he kissed me He'd have God for his father & never want joy
All I want is someone to listen	At starting, is my object. Nay we'll go, Someone had better be prepared for rage, I want to be someone
Sometimes we should slow down and enjoy the lives	From the wisdom of many life-times in my heart, I love him dear, Draining our life energy, its role

2.6 System Evaluation

2.6.1 Design of the Evaluation

In this user evaluation, 15 participants were selected randomly with the average age of 26. To understand the users' engagement and social experience, we have focused on three main directions of the Poetry Mix-up system in this user evaluation. The usability and acceptance of the system, interaction, and social communication using the system, and the possibilities of using the system to preserve the art of the poetry are the three main focuses of this study.

1. *Acceptance of Poetry Mix-up*

    Question—Are users comfortable with Poetry Mix-up?
    Hypothesis—Users would be satisfied with the system regarding the experience
                and the related outputs;
    Example statement 1.1—I like the system;
    Example statement 1.2—I think the generated poetry is related to the input SMS;
    Example statement 1.3—I prefer to see the SMS directly on the screen;
    Example statement 1.4—I prefer generating poetry from the SMS; and
    Example statement 1.5—I felt like I am a poet when using the system.

2. *Social communication using Poetry Mix-up*

    Question—Could Poetry Mix-up be used as a tool for social communication?
    Hypothesis—The system could be used for indirect social communication
    through poetry;
    Example statement 2:1—I think this system could be used to communicate with
                others; and

Example statement 2.2—I think this system could be used as an indirect communication tool with my friends (e.g., blogs, Facebook, and Twitter are used as indirect communication tools).

3. **Preserve poetry culture**

Question—Could Poetry Mix-up be used to preserve the poetry culture?
Hypothesis—The system could preserve the poetry culture;
Example statement 3.1—I think the traditional poetry culture is in danger;
Example statement 3.2—I think this system could help to preserve the poetry culture; and
Example statement 3.3—I would like to communicate with others through poetry.

2.6.2 Results of the Evaluation

Data collected from the survey after using the system is expressed as mean unless otherwise specified. Results of the survey are presented in Tables 2.10 and 2.11. Table 2.10 presents the high-level results according to each section, and Table 2.11 presents the results according to the statements. Of all elements explored in this survey, most of them performed positively in the survey as more than 50% selected the favorable choice to the statements posed. Only statement 1.2 based on generated poetry and input SMS provided a balanced result. A detailed analysis of results is described as follows.

In the aspect of acceptance of Poetry Mix-up, none of the users commented negatively on statement 1.1 that denoted all the participants liked and enjoyed the system. Although the system could not always generate the poem according to the meaning of the input message accurately, some of the participants still provided positive feedbacks. One participant said that it was really nice to see the response corresponding to her SMS. One other user commented that he wondered about the poems generated by the system, and whether they are really meaningful. He felt that the poems are much closer to his feelings. On the other hand, many comments on improvement were received during the user evaluation. For example, the system

Table 2.10 Summarized results of user evaluation based on three main sections

	Negative (%)	Neutral (%)	Positive (%)
Usability	18	28	54
Social communication	8	25	67
Preserve poetry culture	13	29	58

Table 2.11 Detailed results of user evaluation based on individual statements

Statement	Options (%)		
	No	Neutral	Yes
1.1	0	31	69
1.2	37	25	38
1.3	19	31	50
1.4	12	25	63
1.5	19	31	50
2.1	12	19	69
2.2	6	12	82
2.3	6	44	50
3.1	6	31	63
3.2	25	19	56
3.3	6	37	57

still needs more accurate result in understanding the input SMS. One user suggested that it would be better if this system can input and output in other languages as well. The user further commented that rather than outputing a complete poem, it would be better if the system can output poetic phrases for users to create a poem according to his/her creativity.

In the section of social communication using Poetry Mix-up, more than 60% of the participants agreed that poetry could be used as a medium for communicating at present, and they could use the system to communicate with their friends indirectly. Some of the participants suggested that if this system can be published as a free application for people, it would be popular among all the communities. One other suggestion for the improvement was that as a communication media, it would be better if the system could give related images which could provide more emotional value to the poem lines.

In the final section of the questionnaire about preserving poetry culture using the Poetry Mix-up system, as can be seen in Table 2.10, 58% of users agreed that the system provides opportunity to preserve poetry culture. As the results from the study reveal, even though most of the participants believed that the traditional poetry culture is in danger, they would like to communicate with others through poetry. Given below are some of the positive comments from the participants.

> I strongly believe that this system would effectively be used to spread traditional poems
> It is a good way of preserving poetry culture

In addition, another participant commented that the system should understand the different cultural elements in order to generate better poems. However, these comments prove that the application of Poetry Mix-up system into the contemporary culture would be a pleasurable experience while preserving the traditional poetry culture. The high percentage of positive responses indicated that people feel that the system supports social communication and helps to preserve the poetry culture. This is a very significant result since social interaction and poetry are some of the foremost aspirations of Poetry Mix-up.

2.7 Conclusion

In this chapter, we have introduced a conceptual line of reasoning regarding cultural computing. We have responded to the queries of why we need to merge computer technology with culture, whether the computer technology is a culture and in which sense the computers and culture are merged and what are the benefits it may bring to our society. One of our reasonings is that computer technology has travelled beyond being a mere tool to being the most significant part of modern society. We have presented key features in cultural computing in modeling literature: literature regeneration, pervasive experience, mass accessibility, and social connectivity and introduced Poetry Mix-up that features these aspects. According to the results of the system evaluation, our system, which we have developed based on the cultural computing framework, is positively accepted. We are hopeful that these results would open further doors in the discourse in cultural computing.

We will further explore the potential opportunities available for advanced development in this domain while concentrating on strengthening the social connections and narrowing the gaps that are breaching the communications in society. The existing systems have amply justified the achievability of the various approaches in cultural computing and the unlimited space for innovative experiments that would provide interactive cultural experiences. Further developments in this sphere would be a revitalizing immersive experience to the contemporary society, which will eventually reflect on their actual cultural transactions.

Acknowledgments This chapter is a result of a collaborative project with Kening Zhu, Nimesha Ranasinghe, Eng Tat Khoo, Vidyarth Eluppai Srivatsan, Janaka Prasad Wijesena of Mixed Reality Lab, National University of Singapore, Singapore.

References

Amoore L (2005) The global resistance reader. Psychology Press
Bakardjieva M (2003) Virtual togetherness: an everyday-life perspective. Media Cult Soc 25:291–313
Boguraev B, Christopher K (1999) Salience-based content characterisation of text documents. Adv Autom Text Summ 99–110
Carey JW (2008) Communication as culture, revised edition: essays on media and society. Routledge
Cheok AD, Khoo ET, Liu W, Xiao MH, Marini P, Zhang XY (2008) Confucius computer: transforming the future through ancient philosophy. In: ACM SIGGRAPH 2008 new tech demos, ACM, p 10
Geertz C (1973) The interpretation of cultures: selected essays. Basic books

Hannerz U (1992) Cultural complexity: studies in the social organization of meaning. Columbia University Press

Hu J, Bartneck C, Salem B, Rauterberg M (2008) ALICE's adventures in cultural computing. Int J Arts Technol 1:102–118

Manovich L (2001) The language of new media. MIT press

Miller G, Fellbaum C (1998) Wordnet: an electronic lexical database. MIT Press, Cambridge

Pacey A (1983) The culture of technology. MIT press

Song M, Elias T, Martinovic I, Mueller-Wittig W, Chan TKY (2004) Digital heritage application as an edutainment tool. In: Proceedings of the 2004 ACM SIGGRAPH international conference on virtual reality continuum and its applications in industry, ACM, pp 163–67

Song M, Elias T, Müller-Wittig W, Chan TKY (2003) Interacting with the virtually recreated Peranakans. In: Proceedings of the 1st international conference on Computer graphics and interactive techniques in Australasia and South East Asia, ACM, pp 223–ff

Tosa N, Matsuoka S, Thomas H (2004) Inter-culture computing: ZENetic computer. In: ACM SIGGRAPH 2004 emerging technologies, ACM, p 11

Tosa N, Obara H, Minoh M, Matsuoka S (2007) Hitch haiku. In: Proceedings of the 2nd international conference on Digital interactive media in entertainment and arts, ACM, pp 6–7

Williams R (2001) The long revolution. Broadview Press

Chapter 3
Electric and Magnetic User Interfaces for Digital Smell and Taste

Abstract In this chapter, we present how electrical and magnetic user interfaces create or modify taste and smell sensations with new interactions. In the future, these technologies can play a vital role in food consumption, food manufacturing, food-based interactions, and multisensory communication. We provide a detailed review of previous electrical, thermal, and magnetic interfaces in related research area, and then, we present the currently ongoing research works carried out by the author. We also discuss how these technologies can create and modify new interactions for industries such as food, marketing, communication, and computing. In particular, we believe that the future of Internet will not only depend on visual, audio, and tactile stimuli, but also on smell (olfaction) and taste (gustation). Humans would share these stimuli collectively as an experience digitally, like they do with the visual and audio media on the Internet. We want to propose an idea of digital olfaction and gustation as input and output for interaction in creating and experiencing digital representation of foods.

Keywords Digital smell · Digital taste · Magnetic interfaces · Food interaction

3.1 Introduction

Computers and the Internet have both changed people's lifestyles so rapidly in the last few decades. Today, we are moving toward a hyperconnected era where humans and all the electronic devices that we use will be connected together and form a single network. Most of the machines will be also equipped with human senses such as audio, visual, and tactile. Therefore, we believe the next important breakthrough of Internet would be the use of smell and taste digitally. This would include sensing smell and taste information from one location, transferring them over the Internet digitally, and effectively regenerating the signals at the destination.

Since Internet works on digital data, we need the sensors to sense smell and taste information and convert them to digital signals for communication. The destination

© The Author(s) 2016
A.D. Cheok, *Hyperconnectivity*, SpringerBriefs in Human–Computer Interaction,
DOI 10.1007/978-1-4471-7311-3_3

receiving those data needs to be converted from digital signals to analog smell and taste sensations. Therefore, there is a need for smell and taste actuation technologies to be compatible with digital information. Since smell and taste detection sensors and products are already available, actuation becomes the most important. To solve this issue, over the years we have developed and proposed a number of actuation technologies that could regenerate the smell and taste experiences. These interfaces are developed using two main technologies.

Electrical Interfaces—electric sour taste machine and electric smell machine

Magnetic Interfaces—magnetic food, magnetic levitation platform

Electric sour taste interface is an electrical tongue actuator stimulation device, which the user places in their mouth and controlled by the computer, where it can effectively generate sour sensations. Our previous user studies have suggested that by changing the current and frequency, we can also generate salt and bitter sensations. Electric smell interface is an attempt to stimulate smell sensation by stimulating the human olfactory receptors using weak electrical pulses. There will be two thin electrodes placed on the nasal concha for stimulation.

Magnetic food research is focusing on developing edible magnetically reactive foods. Most of the iron-enriched foods that we consume in our daily life are magnetically reactive. Therefore, we are looking to use iron and use some other magnetically reactive metals to mix with foods and make them edible. Then, we will be able to implement new interactions to these foods such as changing the weight of the food, turning, rotating, and levitating.

Magnetic table interface is going to be made with an array of Bitter electromagnets (Bitter 1936) underneath the table. Using the magnetic flux generated from this interface, we will be able to introduce new interactions for cutleries and food such as change of the weight, rotate, and levitate.

We have conceptualized some scenarios for how these smell and taste interfaces would work. Our ideas are Virtual Messenger Menu, Culinary Education, Collaborative Remote Dining, Ambiguous Food, and approximating a service for future food printing at home.

Virtual Messenger Menu: Internet and mobile phone services can be integrated with our smell–taste technologies to provide smell and taste information for their digital contents. For example, when a restaurant introduces a new menu, they can conduct a special promotion through Messenger App using the smell–taste accessories. They can send online coupons to their customers containing smell–taste information for a new dish, and when the customer begins to read this message, he or she can smell or taste the new menu from their accessories. Customers are able to check the restaurant menu using the smell–taste accessory by logging into the diner's homepage, before visiting the restaurant physically. Also for Web site, this technology can be embedded into the site ads.

Culinary Education: Watching a recipe video gives us two sources of information: visual and auditory. In the near future, we could see audiovisual systems that are expanded to utilize smell and taste. You can check your own dish in progress by comparing the taste to the chef's dish. Similarly, we could add new dimensions to food entertainment media. When the lid comes off a steaming pot on your streaming video, you experience the same smell and taste sensations.

New Food Dining Experiences: Using the magnetic table platform and magnetic food, users will be able to experience new food interactions in future. After users order food in the restaurants, they will be able to adjust the weight of the utensils such as spoon, fork, knife, and plates. For example, they will be able to change the weight of these utensils to zero (to simulate zero gravity environment) or negative (negative gravity) where they can levitate them with the foods. Food served in the restaurant can also be magnetically active. This enables adding different properties to the food such as changing the shape and texture of the food dynamically, changing the weight of the food dynamically, vibration, repulsion, and attraction.

Collaborative Remote Dining: We would be able to enhance remote co-dining and co-cooking experience, by translating tastes sense to music notes to record our daily recipe in an interesting way. We call this "taste symphony." By capturing the taste from a dish cooked at one location and reconstructing and delivering in a personalize manner, we envision a simple consumer technology that allows for those lonely individuals to cook meals collaboratively with their children remotely. Through enhancing tastes generated in kitchen, developing a protocol to transmit tastes, and enabling the reconstruction of tastes in a remote collaborative cooking space, humans from all over the world could express their creative nature in the remote co-presence and co-living experience through this new kitchen space.

Ambiguous Food: Sensing occurs between the sender's environment and the media. The sensors can detect smells and tastes from the environment or from specific foods. An example is that the various sensors in a kitchen can measure the smells and tastes currently in the room. The sensed aromas and tastes can be communicated through the Internet after converting them into digital information and actuate on a specific user using the small wearable device. 3D food printing could be the ultimate output, eventually. A chef could use the taste and smell to give quick feedback to an ongoing recipe which when finalized could be added to a 3D printed food. In the future, we would expect a home user to have such devices installed in their homes like normal printers. A user could design his/her own food to be printed and send it to his/her friends' printing device. While constructing the food to save resource, they can experience the food with taste and smell devices. They could even upload this as a work in progress to allow others to quickly sample the food for approval.

The next sections of this paper will discuss the literature related to these interfaces, development details of our new interfaces, and their applicability for various different fields.

3.2 Literature Review of Previous Digital Interfaces for Foods

New user interfaces that we are developing for the smell and taste use electrical energy and magnetic energy. The following subsections detail the previous works related to our research prototypes.

3.2.1 Electrical Interfaces

In one of his experiments, Alessandro Volta put two coins, made of different metals, on both sides of his tongue (up and down) and connected them through a wire. He mentioned that he felt a salty sensation (Volta 1800). In 1976, Plattig and Innitzer were electrically stimulated a single human tongue papilla with a silver electrode using five young subjects (Plattig and Innitzer 1976). They used both negative and positive electrical pulses with a frequency range of 50–800 Hz. The results provided effective responses for the sour taste (22.2%) and some small responses for bitter (3.8%) and salty (1.8%) sensations. When we consider taste, mathematical models of the excitation for chemical stimulation of the taste receptors have been proposed in 1977 (Price and Desimone 1977). Lawless presented metallic taste generation from electrical and chemical stimulation (Lawless et al. 2005). They observed the similarities and differences of stimulation with metals, electrical stimulation, and solutions of divalent salts and ferrous sulfate and investigated sensations that occurred across oral locations using electrical stimulation and different metal anodes and cathodes.

The electrical stimulated sour taste experience was recorded in 1996 from weak electrical current delivered to the surface of the tongue (Lindemann 1996). However, recent results have shown that electrogustronomy relates to an ability to appreciate all the four tastes: sour, sweet, salt, and bitter. The electrogustometry correlated with all four taste qualities was found in 2007 (Ellegård et al. 2007). They proposed that there is a direct depolarizing mode of action of the sensory-neural tongue aspects.

Nakamura and Miyashita have used electricity for augmented gustation (Nakamura and Miyashita 2011). They apply electric current through isotonic drinks and juicy foods to change the taste perception by pulsing voltage and amplitude input.

Researchers have recently produced what they call olfactory hallucinations (Kumar et al. 2012) by placing nodes on the ventral surface of the frontal lobe of children with epilepsy. Eleven out of sixteen patients stated that they were able to smell perceptions.

In most of the olfactory system-related studies examining electrical activity of the olfactory bulb, an adequate olfactory stimulus such as blowing odorous air into the nose has been used as a routine method of activating the olfactory bulb. Only few attempts have been made to do an electrical stimulation of the olfactory system.

Yamamoto has stimulated the human olfactory mucosa by electrical pulse to detect the bulbar potentials (Yamamoto 1961). Electrical stimulation (2 mA, 0.5 ms) of the human olfactory mucosa evoked a change in potential recorded from the frontal sector of the head. During an experiment conducted in 1997, the properties of the olfactory bulb potential evoked by electrical stimulation of the olfactory mucosa were studied in rabbits immobilized with d-tubocurarine (Ishimaru et al. 1997). The evoked potential was a slow negative wave when recorded from the surface of the bulb. In 2002, they concluded that electrical olfactory evoked potential (EOEP) is suitable for electrophysiology (Ishimaru et al. 2002). The relationship between the EOEP and Toyoda and Takagi's perfumist's strip method (Doty 1997), which is a standard Japanese means of psychophysical olfactometry, is investigated. Electrical stimulation via bipolar electrodes (2 mA, 0.5 ms, 300 trials) is feed to the olfactory mucosa. Four channels of EOEP are amplified, filtered (2–250 Hz), and recorded. During electrical stimulation of right or left of the olfactory mucosa evoked an electrical olfactory evoked potential. However, there is no sense of smell occurred.

From the above, the possibility of using non-chemical stimulation methods to stimulate smell and taste sensations digitally can be seen. However, the above-reported studies are conducted mainly in the medical domain (with controlled environments) and are invasive, or only in the experimental stage. Therefore, to achieve electrical and magnetic stimulation methods as a means of actuating the sensations of taste and smell, this research will achieve research breakthroughs in controllability, accuracy, and robustness.

3.2.2   Magnetic Interfaces

Due to the nature of the magnetic fields, direct human interaction is not possible because humans cannot touch or feel them physically. Even though magnetic fields are intangible, they could be transformed into different forms of energies or signals to provide tangible interactions. It is possible to generate attraction, repulsion, actuation, kinaesthetic feelings (Grinder and Bandler 1981), and pressure (Jansen et al. 2010; Weiss et al. 2011) using magnetic fields. Further, magnetic materials can be used to develop interactive user interfaces (Wakita et al. 2011; Frey 2004; Hook et al. 2009).

One of the earlier works of the authors, liquid interface (Karunanayaka et al. 2011), is related to the magnetic table and food research. This was an organic user interface (OUI) (Holman and Vertegaal 2008) that combines Hall effect sensing and actuation through electromagnetically manipulated ferrofluid. The movement of magnets worn on the fingertips, over a surface embedded with a Hall effect sensor array and electromagnets, gives user the ability to interact with the ferrofluid. This system provided a three-dimensional, physically animated response, as well as three-dimensional, spatial-sensing inputs. The vibration of the magnets worn on the

Fig. 3.1 Four different prototypes of the liquid interface system. *Top-left* playing as a piano using a magnetic wand, *top-right* touchless interface waving the hand on top of the surface to create and modify ferrofluid patterns, *bottom-right* direct touch interface that can create and feel ferrofluid bubbles, *bottom-right* playing with piano using a magnetic finger extension

fingertips, produced by the repulsing polarity of the electromagnets, provides the user with haptic feedback. Liquid interface is a multimodal interface with a visual, audio, and haptic experience (see Fig. 3.1). Input and output interactions of this interface are both coupled into a single display. Further, shape changeable surface was developed using a malleable material (ferrofluid) where the user could control and repeat the user interactions. These types of interface will be useful to operate in dynamic environments where the user interface should adapt itself to the external signals.

Haptic mouse (Karunanayaka et al. 2013) (shown in Fig. 3.2) was another similar work done by the authors similar to the magnetic table research. This was a pointing interface for computers, which provides mouse functionalities with near-surface haptic sensations. These functionalities were attained by tracking the 3D position of a neodymium magnet using Hall effect sensors grid and generating like polarity haptic feedback using an array of electromagnets. Haptic mouse couples the near-surface sensing and the haptic actuation together. It brings haptic sensations to 3D spacesSpaces near to the surface which can be considered as a novel experience. Users are able to manipulate the objects in the screen by moving their finger on or above the haptic mouse surface. This added an extra dimension as

Fig. 3.2 Haptic mouse system

the input. Haptic sensations can be felt on top of the surface as well as above the surface. Different vibration pattern-based feedback allows this interface to be used as a haptic display.

3.3 Current and Work in Progress Prototypes

This section will detail the smell, taste, and food research works that are being developed by the authors related to digital actuation of smell and tastes. These interfaces are electric sour taste interface, electric smell interface, magnetic food, and magnetic levitation platform.

3.3.1 Electrical Interfaces

3.3.1.1 Electric Taste Interface

To generate taste sensations digitally, we developed a prototype that can deliver electric current in a controllable and safe manner to a user's tongue. Our approach is shown in Fig. 3.3, where a user places the apparatus across the surface of their tongue. We generate an output from a digital source and apply the electric current, which is then output to the tongue membrane when the tongue makes physical contact with the device. The current travels across the tongue and excites the taste cells that signal the brain that a taste is being sensed.

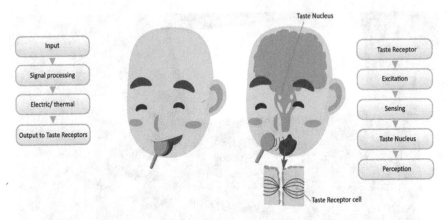

Fig. 3.3 Approach to digital taste stimulation

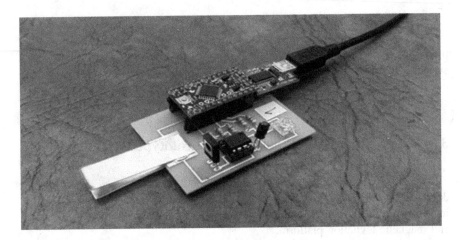

Fig. 3.4 Digital taste interface

To implement the device, we created a digital circuit PCB as shown in Fig. 3.4. The hardware consists of a microcontroller which accepts input from a PC terminal via USB connection. The microcontroller outputs pulse width modulation (PWM) signals. We use this feature to produce square waves of varying frequencies and magnitudes to control the taste interface. The user feels this current simulation with their tongue, and the result produces several kinds of taste sensations. We use a magnitude range of 20–200 µF and a frequency range of 50 Hz–1 kHz.

Because of impedance differences of everyone's tongues, we created an additional part of the circuit that provides a constant current source using an operational amplifier and an NPN transistor. The current output is delivered to the load, the silver tongue electrodes, which are placed on the top and the bottom of the tongue.

Fig. 3.5 Magnitude and frequency results on taste perception

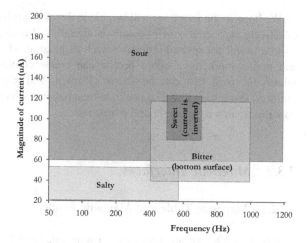

We mounted the electrodes to the PCB at a slight angle using a special silver epoxy that conducts current from the PCB pad to the electrodes.

We conducted a preliminary study across fifteen participants to evaluate the effectiveness of digital taste as a means to stimulate taste. Participants chosen were of good health and reported no taste problems and were instructed not to eat, drink, or smoke two hours before the tests. We were interested in the robustness of such a system, such as sensory adaption, controllability of the tastes within a population, and also the comfort of using this system.

Our study shows (as shown in Fig. 3.5) that some tastes can be effectively actuated (salty, sour, and bitter) across our population of users. Sweetness was also reported but did not have as high of a reported rate as the other three tastes. Users showed some hesitance when placing the device into their mouths due to its appearance.

3.3.1.2   Electric Smell Interface

Instead of using any chemical odors, we hope that by using weak electrical pulse, we can excite the smell receptors and the brain. We are currently developing small bipolar stimulating electrodes that can reach the smell receptors near the olfactory bulb and concha through the nostrils. There are three regions inside the nostrils called superior nasal concha, middle nasal concha, and inferior nasal concha that are nearest to the olfactory receptors where stimulating electrodes could be placed. The placement of electrodes will be done with a help of a medical expert in a way that electrodes would not come off quickly. These electrodes will be controlled by a specially designed circuit that can deliver up to 2 mA of current (according to the previous experiments carried out in the medical field) to the smell-sensitive cells. Currently, we are developing the controller circuit and stimulation electrodes with adjustable parameters for experimenting our idea with users.

We hope in the future we will be able to develop a robust interface where we can effectively regenerate smell sensations digitally. This digital regeneration of smell will be useful for several industries such as gaming, virtual reality, entertainment, and online marketing, where people can create content, information, and food related to smell that can be shared, learned, and experienced. In the medical industry, this research will be useful to treat patients who are suffering from medical conditions such as anosmia and parosmia.

3.3.2   Magnetic Interfaces

3.3.2.1   Magnetic Table and Magnetic Foods

In this research, we are presenting a magnetic object levitation platform with a haptic display where users can interact with objects with changing weights and food that are edible with magnetic properties. One of the main experiments we intend to do using this system is to study the effects of the weight of utensils and food on perceived smell and taste of food. We will configure the proposed platform as a dining table and change the weight of utensils and food by using magnetic fields while eating.

The magnetic table interface will be developed with an array of electromagnets underneath of the table, where we can levitate/move the magnetic objects (utensils/ foods) placed on top of its surface. The proposed platform is shown in Fig. 3.6. This platform utilizes the fundamental physics of magnetic forces-at-a-distance for object levitation. The force produced will repel, attract, vibrate, or levitate the object.

Magnetic table interface needs to generate a very high magnetic field to move and levitate things, and therefore, we will be using Bitter plate electromagnets (Geim 1998). Bitter electromagnets are known for generating extremely strong magnetic fields. In general, the field generated by iron core electromagnets is often

Fig. 3.6 Proposed magnetic table interface

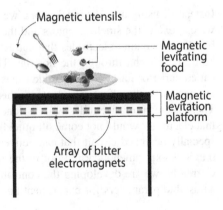

limited to around 2 T, while Bitter coils can produce a very high magnetic field such as 45 T (Bitter 1936). These electromagnets are made by attaching metal plates (e.g., copper) and insulating plates on top of each other in a helix-type structure. This method enables the electromagnet to withstand the immense Lorentz forces created internally. Liquid coolant-based cooling mechanism is needed for these electromagnets to absorb the heat generated and preventing them from melting down while operating.

Further, this interface would be able to create different types of haptic sensations using "like polarity haptics." The haptic sensations that can be felt include attraction, repulsion, and various patterns of vibrations. These sensations can be easily controlled by changing the polarity and frequency of the electromagnets. This technology will be able to provide interactions such as haptics in midair, guide the user to a particular location through a virtual path, provide surface features of 2D and 3D virtual objects, and restrict user to a certain virtual boundary. This magnetic table could also be used as new type of physical interaction display.

In the future, we are aiming to introduce specially created edible magnetic food to be used with this interface. The most iron-enriched food is movable using electromagnets, and we will be using iron and other types of metals that are reactive with external magnetic fields to make these food. Also, we will be testing the food that have permanent magnet inside, which is similar to a fruit or vegetable with a seed(s) inside.

3.4   Discussion

We expect our digital smell and taste interfaces to open up a multitude of new horizons and opportunities for research in the future, including the areas of human computer interfaces, entertainment systems, medical, and wellbeing. Digital controllability of the sensation of taste and smell provides a useful platform for engineers, food designers, and media artists to develop multisensory interactions remotely, including the generation of new virtual tastes and smells for entertainment systems. For scholarly research, this would help bring about answers to exactly what is the language of taste and smell.

The aim of our final prototypes is to develop them as portable and wearable units, therefore enabling the users to wear these interfaces in daily life situations for augmentation. For example, Google Glass promises a better experience of augmented reality unattainable with a smartphone. We can also realize accessories that could be attached to smartphones to actuate taste and smell by placing the end of the apparatus in one's mouth and/or nose. A friend could send you a taste or smell over the Internet by social network, and you could taste or smell it electronically. They could simply input a taste or smell into the phone by text or by selecting presets related to their current experience.

Further, these devices will be able to provide stimulation of a taste and smell from something that cannot exist physically. This could also lead to a breakthrough in molecular gastronomy. Training molecular gastronomers is very difficult for most people, due to the requirement to be trained directly by experts at special facilities. Digital taste and smell systems could facilitate this training through a computer or over the Internet. They could train one's sense of taste and smell and possibly lead to the creation of new kinds of consumer edible delights by quickly prototyping new recipes.

We also believe patients who cannot consume certain ingredients, such as those with diabetes, can digitally experience the tastes of these ingredients (such as sugar) in place of the actual chemicals. Our system could do so by augmenting pre-existing tastes without the danger of the actual chemicals being present in the food. It may also be possible to cancel out certain tastes that people do not like, for instance, bitterness, by adding more sweetness to it, without worrying about consuming too much sugar. This might allow humans to even consume certain foods that were previously unappetizing to eat or to encourage children to eat unpopular foods, such as vegetables, to maintain a healthy lifestyle.

As a new form of entertainment, people could experience flavors from the computer in the form of musical beats for both amusement and recording the notes to store our recipes in an interesting way. In this scenario, taste can be composed like a song. They can be composed to vary over time, for example, a sudden change of taste from salty to sweet, which cannot be achieved using real food. People can make new kinds of recipes using purely digital compositions and post them on a social media site.

Users can create new knowledge using digital taste and smell machines and add pages embedded with flavors similar to adding pictures or sounds to a Webpage. People can rate the experiences by sharing them through another flavor. These experiences can gather to form more and more complex flavors and realize new potentials in gastronomy through our devices. A chef or restaurant owner could introduce a new menu by sending alerts to fans of their creation containing flavor information for the new dishes. When the user opens the message, he or she can taste and smell the new menu from their accessories together with the food image.

3.5 Conclusion

Audio, visual, and haptic fields are well researched. We believe the next challenge is virtual taste and smell using techniques that are currently unattainable using chemical-based methods. Digital taste and smell technologies attempt to actuate taste and smell with electrical and magnetic stimulation non-invasively. This has advantages over chemical stimulation because it is more manageable, and taste and smell can be transmitted directly over the Internet. We believe through this research we can eventually digitally actuate all basic tastes (bitterness, saltiness, sourness, sweetness, umami) and all main smells (putrid, vegetable, floral, woody, minty, fruity) using digital means to actuate and transmit taste and smell information. It could have long-term implications in the future of many disciplines. By using digital taste and smell, we will be able to create new ways to generate content, and new knowledge of food that can be shared, learned, and created in interesting ways previously unattainable with current methods.

References

Bitter F (1936) The design of powerful electromagnets part II. The magnetizing coil. Rev Sci Instrum 7(12):482–488

Doty RL (1997) Practical approaches to clinical olfactory testing, Taste and smell disorders. Thieme, New York, pp 38–51

Ellegård EK, Goldsmith KD, Hay David, Morton RP (2007) Studies on the relationship between electrogustometry and sour taste perception. Auris Nasus Larynx 34:477–480

Frey M (2004) SnOil-A physical display based on ferrofluid

Geim A (1998) Everyone's magnetism. Phys Today 51:36–39

Grinder J, Bandler R (1981) Trance-formations. NeunyUnguistic programming and the structure of hypnosis

Holman D, Vertegaal R (2008) Organic user interfaces: designing computers in any way, shape, or form. Commun ACM 51:48–55

Hook J. Taylor S, Butler A, Villar N, Izadi S (2009) A reconfigurable ferromagnetic input device. In: Proceedings of the 22nd annual ACM symposium on user interface software and technology, ACM, pp 51–54

Ishimaru T, Miwa T, Shimada T, Furukawa M (2002) Electrically stimulated olfactory evoked potential in olfactory disturbance. Ann Otol Rhinol Laryngol 111:518–522

Ishimaru T, Shimada T, Sakumoto M, Miwa T, Kimura Y, Furukawa M (1997) Olfactory evoked potential produced by electrical stimulation of the human olfactory mucosa. Chem Senses 22:77–81

Jansen Y, Karrer T, Borchers T (2010) MudPad: tactile feedback and haptic texture overlay for touch surfaces. In: ACM international conference on interactive tabletops and surfaces, ACM, pp 11–14

Karunanayaka K, Koh JTKV, Naik EB, Cheok AD (2011) Hall effect sensing input and like polarity haptic feedback in the liquid interface system. In: Ambient intelligence, Springer, Berlin

Karunanayaka K, Siriwardana S, Edirisinghe C, Nakatsu R, Gopalakrishnakone P (2013) Haptic mouse magnetic field based near surface haptic and pointing interface. Int J Interact Digit Media 1:8–15

Kumar G, Juhász C, Sood S, Asano E (2012) Olfactory hallucinations elicited by electrical stimulation via subdural electrodes: effects of direct stimulation of olfactory bulb and tract. Epilepsy Behav 24:264–268

Lawless HT, Stevens DA, Chapman KW, Kurtz A (2005) Metallic taste from electrical and chemical stimulation. Chem Senses 30:185–194

Lindemann B (1996) Taste reception. Physiol Rev 76:719–766

Nakamura H, Miyashita H (2011) Augmented gustation using electricity. In: Proceedings of the 2nd augmented human international conference, 34

Plattig K-H, Innitzer J (1976) Taste qualities elicited by electric stimulation of single human tongue papillae. Pflügers Archiv 361:115–120

Price S, Desimone JA (1977) Models of taste receptor cell stimulation. Chem Senses 2:427–456

Volta A (1800) On the electricity excited by the mere contact of conducting substances of different kinds. In a letter from Mr. Alexander Volta, FRS Professor of Natural Philosophy in the University of Pavia, to the Rt. Hon. Sir Joseph Banks, Bart. KBPRS' Philos Trans R Soc Lond 90:403–431

Wakita A, Nakano A, Kobayashi N (2011). Programmable blobs: a rheologic interface for organic shape design. In: Proceedings of the fifth international conference on Tangible, embedded, and embodied interaction, ACM, pp 273–276

Weiss M, Wacharamanotham C, Voelker S, Borchers J (2011) FingerFlux: near-surface haptic feedback on tabletops. In: Proceedings of the 24th annual ACM symposium on User interface software and technology, ACM, pp 615–620

Yamamoto (1961) Olfactory bulb potentials to electrical stimulation of the olfactory mucosa, Jpn J Physiol 11:545–54

Chapter 4
Love and Sex with Robots

Abstract The publication of the book "Love and Sex with Robots," late in 2007 by David Levy, heralded a new era in this somewhat controversial field. Human–robot intimate relationships were no longer pure science fiction but had entered the hallowed halls of serious academic research. Since then, researchers have come up with many implementations of robot companions such as sex robots, emotional robots, humanoid robots, and artificial intelligent systems that can simulate human emotions. Such new technologies contribute to a new dimension of hyperconnectivity, in which human can interact with machines or virtual agents on the Internet on an emotional level, express love and empathy, and form humanistic relationships. This chapter presents a summary of significant activity in this field during the years since that publication, and predicts how the field is likely to develop.

Keywords Human-robot relationships · Lovotics · Sex robots · Kissing machine

4.1 Introduction

Intimate relationships, such as love and sex, between human and machines, especially robots, have been one of the main topics in science fiction. However, this topic has never been treated in academic areas until recently. The topic was raised and discussed by David Levy in his book titled "Love and Sex with Robotics" published in 2007 (Levy 2007a). The book found an eager public in North America who wanted to know more. During the period immediately prior to publication of the book and for a few months afterward, the topic caught the imagination of the media, not just in the USA and Canada but on a worldwide scale. During those months, David Levy gave around 120 interviews, by telephone, e-mail, and in person; to newspapers, magazines, radio, and TV stations; and to electronic media.

© The Author(s) 2016
A.D. Cheok, *Hyperconnectivity*, SpringerBriefs in Human–Computer Interaction,
DOI 10.1007/978-1-4471-7311-3_4

Television interviews included an appearance on The Colbert Report[1]—as well as visits to his home by TV crews from Russia, Canada, Austria, France, Germany, Switzerland, and other countries. There was also, not surprisingly, a flurry of interest from women's magazines, including Elle and Marie Claire. And the coverage in general science publications included articles in IEEE Technology and Society Magazine, MIT Technology Review, Scientific American, and Wired.

In the academic world, there has already been sufficient coverage of the topic to demonstrate rather convincingly that it is of interest not only for mainstream media. An academically rewritten version of the book titled "Intimate Relationships with Artificial Partners" (Levy 2007b) also attracted a lot of media publicity. Conferences on robotics, AI, and other computer science-related subjects began to accept and even invite papers on the subject, and there have thus far been two conferences devoted specifically to Human–Robot Personal Relationships. In 2014, the First International Congress of Love and Sex with Robots was held in Madeira. The academic journals that have since chosen to publish papers on the topic have included: Accountability in Research, AI & Society, Artificial Intelligence, Current Sociology, Ethics and Information Technology, Futures, Industrial Robot, International Journal of Advanced Robotic Systems, International Journal of Social Development, International Journal of Social Robotics, International Journal of Techno ethics, New Media and Society, Phenomenology and the Cognitive Sciences, Philosophy Technology, Social Robotics, Technological Forecasting and Social Change, and various publications from the IEEE, Springer and other highly respected technology stables. One paper, from Victoria University of Wellington, New Zealand, achieved a high profile in the general media when it appeared in 2012 for its entertaining depiction of a future scenario in the red-light district of Amsterdam—a life, in 2050, revolving around android prostitutes "who are clean of sexually transmitted infections (STIs), not smuggled in from Eastern Europe and forced into slavery, the city council will have direct control over android sex workers controlling prices, hours of operations and sexual services." (Yeoman and Mars 2012).

Since the initial burst of media interest late in 2007, there have also been TV documentaries and feature movies in which sex with robots, virtual characters, or with life-sized sex dolls was the dominant theme: Ex Machina (2015), Lars and the Real Girl, Meaning of Robots (which had its premiere at the 2012 Sundance Festival), My Sex Robot, Her (2013), and the BBC TV documentary Guys and Dolls as well as the 2004 remake of The Stepford Wives. This points out that it is the sexual nature of the subject matter which is responsible. Sex Sells.

Following the storm of publicity by the launch of the David Levy's book in 2007 (Levy 2007a), the subject of human–robot romantic and intimate relationships rapidly developed into an academic research discipline in its own right. The subject was named "Lovotics," a term coined during discussions at the National University of Singapore between Adrian David Cheok, Sam Ge and Hooman Samani, and first

---

[1]The Colbert Report, (2008). [TV programme] CC.COM.

mentioned in the literature in 2009 (Nomura et al. 2009). In his PhD thesis in 2011, Adrian David Cheok's student Hooman Samani explored certain aspects of Lovotics and describes the design and development of a hardware platform—a robot—which was capable of experiencing complex and human-like biological and emotional states that were governed by artificial hormones within its system (Samani 2011). Samani's robot was a novel-advanced artificial intelligence system and is described in a little more detail in sections below.

The interest in this field from the academic community resulted, in 2013, in the founding of a journal and e-journal devoted entirely to the subject, whose Editor-in-Chief is Adrian David Cheok. Lovotics (Lovotics Journal) defines its own domain as "Academic Studies of Love and Friendship with Robots" (Fig. 4.1).

4.2   The First Crude Sex Robot

One of the most often asked questions in media interviews with the David Levy in 2007–8 was this: *"How soon do you think the first sex robots will be on the market?"* His consistent response was that the technologies necessary to create a crude sex robot were already available, and therefore, it would probably not be more than 2–3 years before some enterprising entrepreneur(s) put these

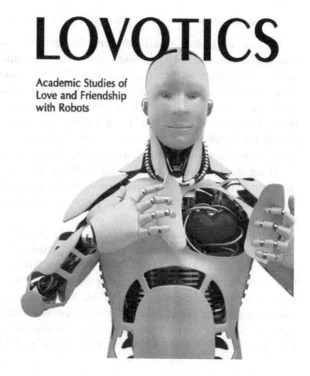

Fig. 4.1 Journal Lovotics, academic studies of love and friendship with robots

LOVOTICS

Academic Studies of
Love and Friendship
with Robots

technologies together. For example, a sex doll with certain parts vibrating and some sexy synthetic speech would be a significant step-up for those customers who have hitherto purchased just a static sex doll. This applies equally to a male bot as to a fem bot—the worldwide commercial success of female vibrators indicates that a male sex doll endowed with a well-designed vibrating penis would be a good start in that direction.

Late in 2009 publicity began to appear in the media about a "sex robot" developed by a New Jersey entrepreneur, Douglas Hines. His Web site www. truecompanion.com proudly proclaimed that "We have been designing "Roxxxy TrueCompanion", your TrueCompanion.com sex robot, for many years, making sure that she: knows your name, your likes and dislikes, can carry on a discussion and expresses her love to you and be your loving friend. She can talk to you, listen to you and feel your touch. She can even have an orgasm!"

Other amazing claims on the truecompanion.com site included:

> She also has a personality which is matched exactly as much as possible to your personality. So she likes what you like, dislikes what you dislike, etc. She also has moods during the day just like real people! She can be sleepy, conversational or she can "be in the mood!"

and

> Roxxxy also has a heartbeat and a circulatory system! The circulatory system helps heat the inside of her body.

and

> She can talk to you about soccer, about your stocks in the stock market, etc.

For millions of men eagerly awaiting the next major technological development that would enhance their sex lives, the announcements about Roxxxy probably seemed too good to be true. And they were! The press launch of Roxxxy took place at the Adult Entertainment Expo in Las Vegas on January 9, 2010, but it posed more questions than it answered. It appeared, for example, that touching Roxxxy's hand caused it to exclaim that "I like holding hands with you," but what does that prove? Only that an electronic sensor was linked to some sort of recorded sound output. It was not a demonstration of the speech technology that would be needed in a talking conversational robot. And furthermore, Hines's behavior during the demonstration prompted the question—how much of the technology was inside Roxxxy and how much in the computer or whatever electronics were located behind the prototype?

The media hype surrounding Hines's launch in Las Vegas seems to have attracted the attention of many prospective customers for Roxxxy's supposedly seductive charms. At the beginning of February 2010, Hines's Web site started to take orders for Roxxxy, advertising the product at a "sale price" of $6495, which it claimed represented a reduction of $500. Accompanying the invitation to place an order, the site also presented a "Master Agreement" that extended to 15 clauses of legalese, covering the purchase of Roxxxy and subscriptions to associated services, but the "RETURNS, REFUNDS AND CANCELLATION POLICY" of that agreement (clause 12.1) made it clear that once production of a customer's Roxxxy commenced, the purchaser could not get any of their money refunded. This begs the question—why would any prospective customer be willing to part with their money without any possibility of recovery, when there had been no public demonstration or independent product review of a fully working Roxxxy that could perform as advertised?

Shortly after truecompanion.com started taking orders for Roxxxy, various news sites posted comments such as:

> Roxxxy won't be available for delivery for several months, but Hines is taking pre-orders through his Web site, TrueCompanion.com, where thousands of men have signed up.

Doubts about Roxxxy persist to this day (July 2015). David Levy wrote an exposé entitled "Roxxxy the 'Sex Robot'—Real or Fake?" and posted it on www. fembotcentral.com. And the Wikipedia entry for Roxxxy (2012) includes the following:

> According to Douglas Hines, Roxxxy garnered about 4000 pre-orders shortly after its AEE reveal in 2010. However, to date, no actual customers have ever surfaced with a Roxxxy doll, and the public has remained skeptical that any commercial Roxxxy dolls have ever been produced.

If it is true that Hines received 4000 preorders, then he would have raked in something over $20 million for those orders, since his Web site demands payment in advance. But as the above extract from the Wikipedia entry indicates, neither Hines himself or any of his customers has demonstrated, in public or to reputable media, the advertised features of Roxxxy actually working. Three years after its "launch," there still appears to be absolutely no sign of a demonstrable product that can talk about Manchester United (as Hines claimed Roxxxy could do) or perform in the other ways that Hines's advertising blurb claimed for Roxxxy.

Despite all the negative aspects of Hines's operation and of the product itself, the launch of Roxxxy at the January 2010 Adult Entertainment Expo can be viewed as some sort of milestone—a vindication of the forecast for a 2- to 3-year time span from late 2007 to the launch of the world's first commercially available sex robot. Hines has proved that there is indeed a significant level of interest in sex robots from the buying public.

4.3 Lovotics

Samani describes the design and development of a robot aimed at imitating the human affection process so as to engender attraction, affection, and at-attachment from human users toward the robot (Samani 2011). Then Samani summarizes the design of the robot thus:

> The artificial intelligence of the robot employs probabilistic mathematical models for the formulation of love. An artificial endocrine system is implemented in the robot by imitating

human endocrine functionalities. Thus, the robot has the capability of experiencing complex and human-like biological and emotional states as governed by the artificial hormones within its system. The robot goes through various affective states during the interaction with the user. It also builds a database of interacting users and keeps the record of the previous interactions and degree of love.

The artificial intelligence of the Lovotics robot includes three modules: The Artificial Endocrine System, which is based on the physiology of love; the Probabilistic Love Assembly, which is based on the psychology of falling in love; and the Affective State Transition, which is based on human emotions. These three modules collaborate to generate realistic emotion-driven behaviors by the robot.

The next four subsections summarize the formulation of love that underpins much of Samani's work, as well as the three software modules of the system mentioned above. The combined effect of these modules is to provide an artificially intelligent model that can display a range of emotions, adjusting its affective state according to the nature and intensity of its interactions with humans. The goal is to develop a robotic system that can exude affection for the user and react appropriately to affection from the user.

4.4   The Formulation of Love

The robot's intimacy software employs parameters derived and quantified from five of the most important reasons for falling in love (Levy 2007a): proximity, repeated exposure, attachment, similarity, and attraction. Intimacy in the robot is thereby related to those same factors that cause humans to fall in love. The robot utilizes audio and haptic channels in order to provide these different types of input which communicate the user's emotional state to the robot (Samani et al. 2010). The audio channel carries data for five audio parameters that characterize emotional cues within a human voice. The haptic channel carries data relating to the user touching the robot—the area of contact between robot and human and the force of that touch.

The Lovotics robot includes mathematical models for those five causal factors of love, creating a mathematical formula to represent each factor as well as a single "overall intimacy" formula which combines these five individual formulae into one. As an example of the five models, the proximity formula incorporates various distances between robot and human that indicate, inter alia, how closely the robot and human are to touching each other, and how close they are emotionally.

4.5   The Probability of Love

The robot algorithm has taken account of the various factors that can engender human love, in order to develop a systematic method for assessing the level of love between a robot and a human. This is achieved by formulating probabilistic mathematical models for these factors, which in turn enable the robot to determine the level of intimacy between humans and robots. These models can be represented in a Bayesian network that depicts the relationship between love and its causal factors. The factors involved in this model include proximity—the physical distance between human and robot; propinquity—spending time with each other; repeated exposure—this can increase familiarity and liking in the other individual; similarity —this is directly related to the feeling of love; etc.

The probabilistic nature of these parameters allows a Bayesian network to be employed to link the parameters to relevant audio, haptic, and location data, leading to an estimate of the probability of love existing between robot and human. For example, audio proximity is employed in the calculations to emulate the effects of physical distance. From the various causal parameters, the system calculates the probabilistic parameters of love, resulting in an appraisal of the level of love between human and robot (Samani and Cheok 2010).

4.6   The Artificial Endocrine System

The human endocrine system is a system of glands that secretes different types of hormones into the bloodstream. The purpose of those hormones is to maintain homeostasis, i.e., to regulate the internal environment of the body in order to keep certain functions stable, such as body temperature, metabolism, and reproductive functions.

The Lovotics artificial endocrine system is based on the human endocrine system, employing artificial hormones to create a simulation of the human system. The artificial hormones are software simulations of those human hormones, which are related to the emotions—Dopamine, Serotonin, Endorphin and Oxytocin, inter alia. The levels of these artificial hormones change dynamically due to the robot's interactions with users and according to its awareness of its emotional and physical circumstances.

4.7   The Affective State Transmission System

The affective state of the Lovotics robot depends largely on the various inputs it receives that are caused by its interactions with humans. Every interaction provides input data that is mapped onto a combination of six basic emotional parameters: happiness, sadness, disgust, surprise, anger, and fear. These six emotions are widely employed and described in the emotion literature.

The manner in which the robot's emotional state changes with the various inputs it receives is controlled by a model of emotion referred to as Affective State Transition (Samani and Cheok 2010). The Lovotics robot has a novel transition system which governs the immediate emotional changes in the robot. Their transition system functions in collaboration with the "probabilistic love assembly" module in order to control the overall emotional state of the robot. The short-term affective state of the robot is thereby transformed repeatedly into other affective states which are determined by the robot's previous affective states, its current mood, and the influences of the various input data it received during its interactions with humans, including audio and touch, and with its environment. For example, temperature could be one environmental input that might be programmed to influence the robot's affective state, if it "dislikes" being cold.

4.8 The Kissenger

In order for robots, such as the Lovotics robot, to have realistic physical interactions with humans, technology needs to be developed for human—machine kissing. In order to address this issue, Adrian David Cheok and his research team in Mixed Reality Laboratory has developed a kissing robot messenger called "Kissenger" (Fig. 4.2) (Cheok et al. 2016).

We live in a global era, and more and more couples and families are apart due to work and business. New technologies are often employed to help us feel connected to those we care about, through an increasing interest in touch and feeling communication between humans in the human–computer interaction community. Research such as "Hugvie" (Kuwamura et al. 2013) and the "Hug over a Distance"

Fig. 4.2 Concept of kiss communication

project (Mueller et al. 2005) tested the feasibilities of telepresence and intimacy technology. However, these are big, bulky, and impractical.

Some commercial work such as "The HugShirt"[2] (2002) and "Huggy Pajama" (Teh et al. 2008) explores hugging in remote with love ones using wearable fashion technology. But these still lack a proper interface for "abstracted presence." Thus, Kissenger proposes a new system to feel the real presence using communication over Internet for humans or robots.

Kissing is one of the most important modes of human communication as it is a universal expression of intimacy. People deeply feel positive emotions such as respect, greeting, farewell, good luck, romantic affection, and/or sexual desire through the physical joining or touching of lips by one individual on another individual's cheek, forehead, etc. (Millstein et al. 1993). Regular physical contact such as kissing is the key to maintaining intimacy in human relationships. Studies have shown that couples who kiss more frequently have higher romantic satisfaction and lower stress level (Floyd et al. 2009).

The first Kissenger device developed by Mixed Reality Laboratory was led by Adrian David Cheok and was unveiled at the Designing Interactive Systems Conference in Newcastle in June 2012 (Samani et al. 2012). It would be possible to integrate the Kissenger technology into a sex robot but initially its use will be in products for enabling family members, friends, and lovers to kiss each other via the Internet.

The Kissenger employed soft, pressure sensitive, vibrating silicone lips which, in the early prototypes, stood out from the surface of a smooth plastic casing-shaped somewhat like a human head. Those early prototypes have since been replaced by a version for mobile phones.

Considering this missing dimension in today's communication technologies, Kissenger aims to design a new device to facilitate the exchange of emotional content to feel a closer sense of presence between people who are physically separated, thus integrating their interpersonal relationships further.

When a user kisses the device on its lips, the changes in shape of the lips are detected by sensors and the resulting data is transmitted over the Internet to a receiving Kissenger, which converts the data back to lip shapes. This reproduces the changes in the kisser's lip shape, changes which are felt by the kisser's partner.

The Kissenger technology could perhaps be enhanced with an idea from a rather more ambitious haptic device of the same ilk which has been developed in Tokyo at the Kajimoto Laboratory in the University of Electro-Technology. Their invention is a French-kissing device (Takahashi et al. 2011), whose prototypes are not yet at a stage where they are likely to inspire erotic thoughts, being based on a straw-like tube that moves when in contact with a user's tongue. But we can expect to see an enhanced form of this idea in a future version of the Kissenger and similar inventions—enhancements under consideration at the Kajimoto Laboratory include adding taste, breath, and moistness to the experience.

---

[2]http://cutecircuit.com/the-hug-shirt/.

During a kiss, along with its strong emotional and affectionate connections, a series of physical interactions takes place. The touch of the lips exchanges the pressure, softness, and warmth of each lip in a convincing way. The inventers of Kissenger approached this design problem carefully, given the intimate nature of the interaction and iteratively designed Kissenger which consists of two paired devices that can send and receive kisses simultaneously as shown in concept images (Figs. 4.3 and 4.4).

After studying the biological and psychological parameters of a kiss, a series of exploratory form factors were drawn to help visualize the possible interfaces. Figure 4.5 shows some of our initial concept designs. At this stage, they looked for designing a system that effectively transmits the same sensation of kiss to one another. The one key issue was that the use of the device should be comfortable and not distract or obstruct the natural interaction of the kiss. Hence, they decided to integrate the initial concept design for a lip-like portable device with a minimalistic shape. However, one of the main concerns was the lip needed to be equipped with sensors and actuators. Hence, they looked into the possible technologies and sizes which could be fit into the form factor of the device. Figure 4.6 shows the 3D depiction of the proposed device with the new shape which can attach to a smartphone, allowing a video call and virtual kiss simultaneously.

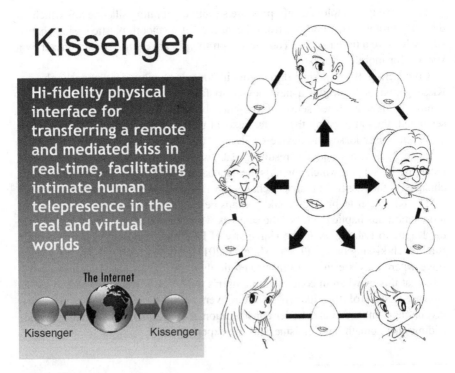

Fig. 4.3 Kissenger usage scenario A

Fig. 4.4 Kissenger usage scenario B

4.8.1 Design Features

The interaction mechanism for Kissenger was devised with a number of features that make kiss communication between two users more meaningful. The system consists of following key features:

- Lip sensor push and pull reverse feedback for kiss behavior.
- Real-time Internet transmission of haptic force data.
- Sending scents.
- Feeling LED light color communication (red, green, blue, yellow, pink, and white).
- Mobile app for kiss communication with video chat.
- One-to-one pair and one-to-many user connections.
- Scent tank changes the scent to suit the partners.
- Soft silicon cover made with gel for kiss communication.

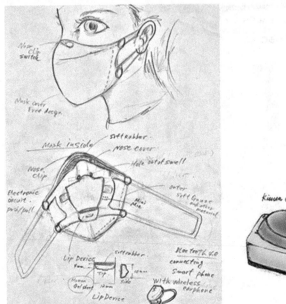

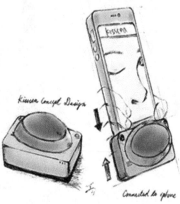

Fig. 4.5 Preliminary concept design of Kissenger

Fig. 4.6 New design of Kissenger which can attach to a mobile phone

4.8.2 Design Flow

The hardware design of Kissenger (Fig. 4.7) with all the features listed above specifies the use of force sensors, linear actuators, a RGB LED, a scent tank, and an audio connector in the Kissenger design flow. Their design flow is as follows.

4.8.2.1 Input Kiss Sensing

The lip surface is made of a soft flexible material to resemble the texture of human lip. An array of force sensors is embedded below the surface of the lip to measure the dynamic forces exerted by different points of the user's lips. The system also can be used during a video chat with another person, or for kissing a robot or a virtual 3D character.

4.8.2.2 Control and Transmission

Kissenger uses a microcontroller in the device to control the sensors and actuators. The device connects to a mobile phone through the Kissenger app, which connects to another user over the Internet (Fig. 4.8). The microcontroller reads the force sensors and sends the force data to the phone. This data is then transmitted over the Internet in real time and received by the partner's device. A bilateral haptic

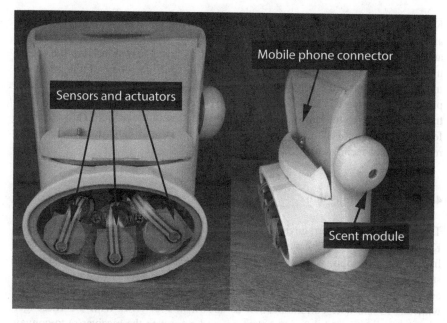

Fig. 4.7 Key design features of Kissenger

Fig. 4.8 Kissenger device
connected to iPhone app

controller is implemented locally to control the output forces of the actuators to generate kiss sensations. The controller is designed such that both users feel the same contact force on their lips simultaneously. The interaction is bidirectional as the user can send and receive a kiss at the same time.

4.8.2.3 Output Kiss Actuation

Kiss sensations are produced by the positional changes of an array of linear actuators. Simultaneously, the scent module emits a scent containing love pheromone and the LED changes color to depict different moods. Pheromones are the scents used in Kissenger that are capable of acting outside the body of the secreting individual to impact the behavior of the receiving individual giving the feel of real presence of the partner. The shape and size of the lip covers hide the inner electronics that go into the sensing, control, and actuation of the device. Thus, all these features make the user more amicable to this device and helps evoke emotional responses and feelings for kiss communication.

4.8.2.4 Communication

Two or more Kissenger devices are wirelessly connected to each other via the Kissenger mobile app. Users can sign up for an account, search, and connect to their friends using the app. When a user starts a video chat with a friend, the application starts to send and receive force data from the Kissenger device. One of the unique added features of the app is that it allows one-to-many user communication along with one-to-one user communication as shown in Fig. 4.10. With the Kissenger app, the user can send different colors or send a scent to the receiver(s) to convey their mood. Figure 4.9 shows a user interacting with the Kissenger device.

Fig. 4.9 A user interacting with Kissenger

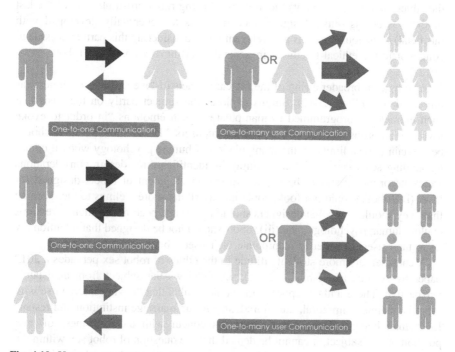

Fig. 4.10 User communication via Kissenger app

An assessment of the new proposed shape and its implementation was conducted with a wide variety of people including researchers not involved in our project, mall shoppers, and friends over a period of time with around fifty people from different cultural backgrounds, age, and sexes participated in the evaluation process and provided feedback for the proposed shape and features. The major feedback is to integrate the size to make it more portable and user-friendly and provide the room for asynchronous kissing. There is the ability for the device to store a kiss that can be read at a later time on which the researchers will be working in the future for the social impact of this project.

4.9 The Ethical and Legal Debate

The ethics of robot sex were first aired in an academic forum at the EURON Workshop on Roboethics in 2006 (Levy 2006a, b, c). The following year David Levy has discussed five aspects of the ethics of robot prostitution at an IEEE conference in Rome (Levy and Loebner 2007): the ethics of making robot prostitutes available for general use; the ethics vis à vis oneself and society in general, of using robot prostitutes; the ethics vis à vis one's partner or spouse, of using robot prostitutes; the ethics vis à vis human sex workers, of using robot prostitutes; and the ethics vis à vis the sexbots themselves, of using robot prostitutes. Since the last of these issues is only of significance if robots are eventually developed with (artificial) consciousness, it is also relevant when considering this particular issue to contemplate the ethical treatment in general of artificially conscious robots (Levy 2012).

A somewhat broader airing of the ethical impacts of love and sex machines was presented by Sullins (2012). Sullins explores the subject partly on the basis that such entities are programmed to manipulate human emotions "in order to evoke loving or amorous reactions from their human users." He submits that there should be "certain ethical limits on the manipulation of human psychology when it comes to building sex robots," and accordingly he identifies three design considerations which he proposes should be applied to the development of robots designed for love: (i) Robots should not fool people into ascribing more feelings to the machine than they should; (ii) robot designers should be circumspect in how their inventions exploit human psychology; and (iii) robots should not be designed that intentionally lie to their users in order to manipulate their user's behavior.

A considerably more strident attitude to the ethics of robot sex pervades a 2012 paper by Amuda and Ismaila (2012), which views the subject from an Islamic perspective. These authors appear to have no doubts that "having intercourse with robot is unethical, immoral, uncultured, slap to the marriage institution and respect for human being." While many might not concur with the robustness of their position on the subject, it cannot be denied that the question of robot sex within the confines of marriage, or indeed within any existing human sexual relationship, is a serious issue. The question most often asked of the present author in media interviews has been: "Is it cheating for someone who is married or in a committed relationship to have sex with a robot?"

In this author's opinion, the answer is a resounding "No." A partner or spouse who has sex with a robot is no more guilty of cheating on their other half than are any of the tens of millions of women who use a vibrator. But not everyone agrees with this position, and in parallel with the possibility that sex with a robot should be regarded as cheating on one's spouse, there comes an interesting legal question which has been flagged by the California lawyer Ziaja (2011). Could a sex robot be legally regarded as the enticing protagonist in a lawsuit brought for the enticement of one's spouse? In the eight states of the USA where this type of law is still on the statute books, where they are called amatory or "heart balm" laws, Ziaja questions whether a sex robot could be held to be the cause, or a contributing cause, to the breakdown and dissolution of a marriage, and if so, who should be held legally liable to pay whatever damages a court might assess? Ziaja suggests a few obvious possible culprits for cases of enticement by a robot: the robot's inventor, its manufacturer, its owner, or even the robot itself. But the attribution of liability for a wrong wrought by a robot is an extremely complex issue, one which this author believes will not be adequately solved in the foreseeable future. Instead, it has been suggested (Levy 2012) that robot wrongs could be compensated by an insurance scheme, much akin to that which works well for automobiles and other vehicles.

The only form of punishment considered by Ziaja for transgressing the American heart balm laws is to compensate the plaintiff, which is a notion that pales into insignificance when compared to the punishments discussed by Amuda and Tijani. They point out that, under Sharia law, judges are permitted to invoke lashes or even capital punishment for having sex with a robot, provided there is sufficient credible evidence of the crime (Ziaja 2011). "To this study, death penalty by hanging may not be applicable and implemented unless there are enough and credible evidences to justify the death by hanging of robot fornicator or adulterer."

Ziaja's paper largely avoids discussing punishment in relation to enticement cases in which a robot is the protagonist, preferring to prevent the problem from occurring by having robots designed in such a way as to incorporate feelings of heartbreak together with the goal of caring for those in its owner's circle of friends and relatives.

> "In order for robots to enter into human romantic relationships in a way that is consistent with the values underlying the heart balm torts, it may also need to experience heartache and empathy as we do." Ziaja's position thus supports that of John Sullins.

An in-depth consideration of whether or not human–humanoid sexual interactions should be legally regulated was discussed by Anna Russell in Computer Law & Security Review (Russell 2009). The very fact that such a discussion should appear in the pages of a respected legal journal points to the seriousness with which the legal profession is viewing the legal implications of the human–robot relationships of the future. Russell suggests that:

> Regulation of human–humanoid sexual interaction either by the state or federal government will be sought when the level of interaction either (1) mimics human sexual interactions

currently regulated or (2) will create a social harm if the interaction is not regulated ... currently, in places where humans are using robots for pleasure in a sexual way that pleasure is either not regulated or is regulated in the way the use of any sexual device may be regulated

but that when more advanced robots/humanoids are used for sexual pleasure, "then in many places, traditional norms and social mores will be challenged, prompting the development of state regulation. Will such regulation, then, be at odds with accepted notions of rights and freedoms?"

Russell then delves further into the question of how regulation of human–humanoid sexual encounters would work and highlights some of the questions that will arise, including:

How many rights will humans allow if humanoids clamor for sexual freedoms? How will humanoids be punished for sexual transgressions? Will humanoids need legal protection from the abuse of human sexual proclivities?

Russell's conclusion is a call for the

... early discussion of the ramifications of a future species' demand for legal rights. . . the legal profession should develop legal arguments before attest case occurs in order to avoid the illogic and danger of arguments that stem from species bias.

In 2011, the MIT Technology Review conducted a poll on people's attitudes to the idea of loving a robot. 19% of those questioned indicated that they believed they could love a robot, 45% said "No" and 36% responded "Maybe." When it came to a question of whether or not people believed that robots could love humans, 36% said "Yes," only 23% responded "No," and 41% "Maybe." So already the idea of human–robot love was taking root as a serious proposition.

In a later poll, one about robot sex rather than robot love, which was conducted in February 2013 by The Huffington Post and YouGov among 1000 American adults, 9% of respondents indicated that they would have sex with a robot, and 42% opined that robot sex would constitute cheating on one's human partner (31% said "No" to the cheating question, while 26% said they were uncertain). This can be taken as further evidence that a significant portion of the population already regards robot sex as a serious subject. Just how serious can perhaps be judged by a news story that hit the media in March 2013 about an online auction for the virginity of a Brazilian sex doll called Valentina (Gates, 26) which was inspired by a 20-year-old Brazilian woman, Catarina Migliorini, who had auctioned her own virginity for $780,000 (sold to a Japanese buyer). True, a sex doll is only an inanimate product, lacking all the interactive capabilities of the sex robots of the future. But the level of interest demonstrated by this news story bodes well for the commercial possibilities of sex robots.

For the Brazilian sex doll auction, the online retailer Sexônico offered a complete romantic package for the successful bidder, which included a one-night stay with Valentina in the Presidential Suite at the Swing Motel in Sao Paulo, a candlelit champagne dinner, an aromatic bath with rose petals, and a digital camera to capture the action. If the successful bidder lived outside Sao Paulo, Sexônico also offered to provide a round-trip air ticket. Valentina's charms were not able to match the great commercial success of Ms Migliorini, but considering that most sex dolls retail at prices in the range $5000–$10,000 the final bid of $105,000 was still a good result for Sexônico, not to mention the value of all the media exposure they attracted.

4.10 Robot Love

In parallel with the developments we have discussed in the field of robot sex and teledildonics, there is a continuing and burgeoning research interest in robot love. Among the fundamental conditions for engendering human love, physical appearance and attractiveness rank highly. The translation of these conditions to the field of robotics has a champion in Professor Hiroshi Ishiguro, whose research teams are based at the Graduate School of Engineering Science at Osaka University and at the Hiroshi Ishiguro Laboratory in the Advanced Telecommunications Research Institute International in Kyoto.

Ishiguro is famous for, inter alia, the amazingly lifelike robots he has developed in various human images (Hofilena 2013). These include one in his own image which is sometimes sent to deliver his lectures when he is too busy to do so himself. Another of his robots, called "Geminoid-F," is made in the image of an attractive young woman who can blink, respond to eye contact, and recognize and respond to body language (Torres 2013). Ishiguro is encouraged in this aspect of his work by his conviction that Japanese men are more prone than are Western men to develop amorous feelings toward such robots because, in Japan, with the influence of the Shinto religion, "we believe that everything has a soul and therefore we don't hesitate to create human-like robots."

Another strand of Ishiguro's research into artificially engendering feelings of love in humans is concerned with promoting romantic forms of communication. The "Hugvie" (Kuwamura 2013) is a huggable pillow, shaped in a somewhat human form, that is held by a user close to their body while they speak to their human partners via their mobile phone, located in a pocket in the Hugvie's head. The Hugvie incorporates a vibrator to simulate a heartbeat, and the vibrations emanating from it are synchronized with the sounds of the partner's voice. This allows the simulated heartbeat to be changed according to the volume of the partner's voice, with the result that the listening user feels as though they are close to their partner. The comfort felt by holding the cushion, the sense of hugging one's partner, hearing one's partner's voice close to one's ear, and the simulated heartbeat aligned with that voice, all these combine to create a sense that the partner is in some way present, which in turn intensifies the listener's feelings of emotional attraction for their partner. Ishiguro expects this intensified affinity to increase the sense of intimacy between couples who are communicating through their respective Hugvie. Ishiguro shared in a breakthrough study that the Hugvie could decrease blood cortisol levels, therefore reducing stress (Sumioka et al. 2013). Integrating the

Hugvie technology into the design of an amorous robot might therefore enable a human user of such a robot to experience an enhanced feeling of a humanlike presence and a greater sense of intimacy from and for the robot.

Yet another direction of Ishiguro's research into having a robot engender emotions in humans is his investigation of the emotional effects, on a human user, of different facial expressions exhibited by a robot (Nishio et al. 2012). That research is currently in its early stages but there is already some indication that it will be possible for robots, by their own facial expressions, to affect a user's emotional state. Emotional facial expression is also a hot topic at the MIT Media Laboratory, where the Nexi robot was developed (Allman 2009).

4.11 Predictions

4.11.1 Robot Sex

Clearly, a significant sector of the public is now ready for the advent of commercially available sex robots, and the public's interest in and appetite for such products seems to be growing steadily. We have noticed a steady increase in the number of requests for media interviews on the subject during the past two years. Also growing steadily is the interest within the academic research community.

In our opinion, nothing has occurred since the publication of Love and Sex with Robots to cast doubt on his 2007 prediction that sophisticated sex robots would be commercially available by the middle of this century. On the contrary, the increase in academic interest in this field has reinforced David Levy's conviction regarding that time frame.

What will be the next significant steps in this field? Intelligent electronic sex toys are gaining in popularity, for example the Sasi Vibrator, which "comes preloaded with sensual intelligence which learns movements you like, specifically tailoring a unique experience by remembering movements that suit you." and the "Love Glider Penetration Machine" which can be purchased from Amazon.com at around $700 and which is claimed to "give you the most comfortable stimulating ride you will ever have!" The Amazon Web site also offers a very much more primitive looking sex machine at around $800, a machine of the type seen in many variations on the specialist site www.fuckingmachines.com, and which "supports multiple positions, has adjustable speeds, strong power, remote control."

Another research direction that perhaps offers even greater commercial potential comes from a combination of augmented reality with digital surrogates ("Dirrogates") of porn stars. A recent posting by DeSouza (2015) posits that the 3D printing of human body parts will enable the downloading, from "hard-drives in Hollywood studios" of "full body digital model and 'performance capture' files of actors and actresses." DeSouza continues:

With 3D printing of human body parts now possible and blue prints coming online with full mechanical assembly instructions, the other kind of sexbot is possible. It won't be long before the 3D laser-scanned blueprint of a porn star sexbot will be available for licensing and home printing, at which point, the average person will willingly transition to trans human status once the 'buy now' button has been clicked.

If we look at Digital Surrogate Sexbot technology, which is a progression of interactive porn, we can see the technology to create such Dirrogate sexbots exists today, and better iterations will come about in the next couple of years. Augmented reality hardware when married to wearable technology such as "fundawear" (2013) and a photo-realistic Dirrogate driven by perf-captured libraries of porn stars under software (AI) control can bring endless sessions of sexual pleasure to males and females.

Fundawear is a prime example of the increase in popularity of intelligent electronic sex toys and teledildonic devices. It is a wearable technology project currently under development by the condom manufacturer Durex, which allows lovers to stimulate their partner's underwear via their respective mobile phones. Such products seem likely to benefit from the increased academic interest in Lovotics, which will surely lead to at least some of the academic research in this field being spun off into commercial development and manufacturing ventures. And the more prolific such products become in the market place, the more the interest in them and in fully fledged sex robots will grow. How long will it be before we see a commercially available sexbot much more sophisticated than Roxxxy? Almost certainly within the next five years.

4.11.2 Robot Love

The past five years has seen a surge of interest in research projects aimed at different aspects of love-with-robots. One aspect is concerned with enabling humans to convey amorous feelings to artificial partners, or to remotely located human partners with whom they communicate by artificial means (i.e., technology). Another aspect works in the opposite direction, enabling artificial partners to exhibit their artificial feelings, including love, to human partners. Some of this research has already demonstrated promising results, for example the experiments conducted with Hugvie by Ishiguro and his team in Japan. They plan further research with the Hugvie to investigate how vibration can further enhance the feeling of presence experienced by a user. Additionally, they plan to employ tactile sensors to monitor the emotional state of a user, which will provide feedback for the Hugvie and thereby enhance its ability to influence a user's emotions. Ishiguro's team has already found that hugging and holding such robots *"is an effective way for strongly feeling the existence of a partner."*

Another domain to become an important catalyst for the development of human–robot emotional relationships is what might be called girlfriend/boyfriend games. An example of this type of game is "Love Plus," which was first released in 2009 for the Nintendo DS games console, and subsequently upgraded for re-release. A recent (February 2013) article describes the relationship between a 35-year-old Tokyo engineer, Osamu Kozaki, and his girlfriend Rinko Kobayakawa (Belford 2013). When she sends him a message

> … his day brightens up. The relationship started more than three years ago, when Kobayakawa was a prickly 16-year-old working in her school library, a quiet girl who shut out the world with a pair of earphones that blasted punk music.

Kozaki describes his girlfriend's personality as being

> … the kind of girl who starts out hostile but whose heart gradually grows warmer. And that's what has happened; over time, Kobayakawa has changed. These days, she spends much of her day sending affectionate missives to her boyfriend, inviting him on dates, or seeking his opinion when she wants to buy a new dress or try a new hairstyle.

But while Kozaki has aged, Kobayakawa has not. After three years, she is still 16. She always will be. That is because she is a simulation; Kobayakawa only exists inside a computer.

Kozaki's girlfriend has never been born. She will never die. Technically, she has never lived. She may be deleted, but Kozaki would never let that happen.

Because he is "in love."

4.12 Conclusion

In this chapter, we discussed the possibility of human robot intimate relationships and humanoid robot sex. We detailed Lovotics, which is a new research field that study emotions of robots with an artificial endocrine system capable of simulating love. We also presented the design and principle of Kissenger, an interactive device that provides a physical interface for transmitting a kiss between two remotely connected people. Finally, we have discussed ethical and legal background and future predictions of love and sex with robots.

References

Allman T (2009) The Nexi robot. House Press, Norwood
Amuda YJ, Tijani IB (2012) Ethical and legal implications of sex robot: an islamic perspective. OIDA Int J Sustain Devel 3(06):19–28
Belford A (2013) That's not a droid. That's my girlfriend. The Global mail. Retrieved from www.theglobalmail.org/feature/thats-not-a-droid-thats-mygirlfriend/560/, 21 Feb 2013
Cheok AD, Levy D, Karunanayaka K, Nishiguchi S, Zhang EY (2016) Lovotics: love and sex with robots. IPSJ J (Special Issue) 57(2)
Desouza C (2015) Sexbots, ethics, and transhumans. Serious & Wonder. from http://www.seriouswonder.com/sexbots-ethics-and-transhumans/
Floyd K, Boren JP, Hannawa AF, Hesse C, McEwan B, Veksler AE (2009) Kissing in marital and cohabiting relationships: effects on blood lipids, stress, and relationship satisfaction. West J Commun 73(2):113–133

Hofilena J (2013) Japanese robotics scientist Hiroshi Ishiguro unveils body-double robot. The Japan Daily Press. Retrieved from http://japandailypress.com/japanese-robotics-scientist-hiroshi-ishiguro-unveils-body-double-robot-1730686/

Kuwamura K, Sakai K, Minato T, Nishino S, Ishiguro H (2013) Hugvie: A medium that fosters love. Paper presented at the RO-MAN, 2013 IEEE

Levy D (2006a) A history of machines with sexual functions: past, present and robot. EURON workshop on roboethics, Genoa

Levy D (2006b) Emotional relationships with robotic companions. EURON workshop on roboethics, Genoa

Levy D (2006c) Marriage and sex with robots. EURON workshop on roboethics, Genoa

Levy D (2007a) Love and sex with robots: the evolution of human-robot relationships. Harper Collins

Levy D (2007b) Intimate Relationships with Artificial Partners. PhD Thesis, University of Maastricht, Netherlands.

Levy D, Loebner H (2007) Robot prostitutes as alternatives to human sex workers

Levy D (2012) When robots do wrong. Paper presented at the conference on computing and entertainment Kathmandu

Millstein SG, Petersen AC, Nightingale EO (1993) Promoting the health of adolescents. Oxford University Press

Mueller FF, Vetere F, Gibbs MR, Kjeldskov J, Pedell S, Howard S (2005) Hug over a distance. Paper presented at the CHI'05 extended abstracts on Human factors in computings systems, ACM

Nishio S, Taura K, Ishiguro H (2012) Regulating emotion by facial feedback from teleoperated android robot. In: Social robotics. Springer, Berlin, pp 388–397

Nomura S, Soon J, Samani HA, Godage I, Narangoda M, Cheok AD, Katai O (2009) Feasibility of social interfaces based on tactile senses for caring communication. Paper presented at the the 8th international workshop on SID

Russell AC (2009) Blurring the love lines: The legal implications of intimacy with machines. Computer Law & Security Review 25(5): 455–463

Samani HA (2011) Lovotics: love + robotics, sentimental robot with affective artificial intelligence

Samani HA, Cheok AD (2010) Probability of love between robots and humans. Paper presented at the 2010 IEEE/RSJ international conference on intelligent robots and systems (IROS)

Samani HA, Cheok AD, Ngiap FW, Nagpal A, Qiu M (2010) Towards a formulation of love in human-robot interaction. Paper presented at the RO-MAN, 2010 IEEE

Samani HA, Parsani R, Rodriguez LT, Saadatian E, Dissanayake KH, Cheok AD (2012) Kissenger: design of a kiss transmission device. Paper presented at the proceedings of the designing interactive systems conference

Sullins JP (2012) Robots, love, and sex: the ethics of building a love machine. IEEE Trans Affect Comput 3(4):398–409

Sumioka H, Nakae A, Kanai R, Ishiguro H (2013) Huggable communication medium decreases cortisol levels. Sci Rep 3

Takahashi N, Kuniyasu Y, Sato M, Fukushima S, Furukaw M, Hashimoto Y, Kajimoto H (2011) A remote haptic communication device that evokes a feeling of kiss. Interaction 2.

Teh JKS, Cheok AD, Peiris RL, Choi Y, Thuong V, Lai S (2008) Huggy Pajama: a mobile parent and child hugging communication system. Paper presented at the proceedings of the 7th international conference on interaction design and children

Torres I (2013) Japanese inventors create realistic female 'love bot'. The Japan Daily Press. Retrieved from http://japandailypress.com/japanese-inventors-create-realistic-female-love-bot-2825990/

Yeoman I, Mars M (2012) Robots, men and sex tourism. Futures 44(4):365–371

Ziaja S (2011) Homewrecker 2.0: an exploration of liability for Heart balm torts involving AI Humanoid consorts. Soc Robot. Springer, Berlin, pp 114–124

Chapter 5
Social Impact of Hyperconnectivity

Keywords Human connections · Information overload · Learning and Education · Smart strategies and governance

5.1 Connected Is not New to Society

A personal perspective by Chamari Edirisinghe

I remember living in a quiet suburb where middle-class working families resided next door to each other. Our house was separated from the side streets; thus, our immediate neighbors are not adjacent. I remember the social interactions of my mother, who was never overtly friendly or social, yet kind and considerate. She never intruded on other peoples' businesses and did not care much for the gossip in that neighborhood, where social status is considered a visual presence. When my mother passed away recently, all my neighbors could recall was her quiet support and friendship, and how connected the neighbors were with her. I knew my mother as an introverted individual, who did not prefer crowds, but all my neighbors saw was the connections, and the networks she built or was in.

Society is that, a formation of connections, connections formed through interactions, thus connected is not a new concept to the society. It is an everyday occurrence, a part of the human nature. People prefer to connect with like-minded individuals or groups, however; the interactions are widespread with individuals and groups from all walks of life. Christakis (2013) states that connections carry other aspects with it such as communication, cooperation, social learning, and even violence.

Each connection generates cooperation, which defines the meaning and boundaries of the connection. When individuals are connected, they form a network

© The Author(s) 2016
A.D. Cheok, *Hyperconnectivity*, SpringerBriefs in Human–Computer Interaction,
DOI 10.1007/978-1-4471-7311-3_5

that leads to interrelated cooperations. These interrelated connections provide a perspective on the inner workings of a society. These are the relations that build communities, gathering together similar-minded individuals or dissimilar individuals with common goals. The cooperation among people creates wealth that is beyond measures.

Like my mother, we all define our own connections. Whether we are having a one-to-one conversation or in a group discussion, our connections are defined by our participation, objectives, and conversation strategy. Our participation in any form of a conversation is a product of our interest in the conversation and the consciousness of our obligations as human beings. The society is produced out of participation, and our participation builds a bridge which gives us the liberty to decide how our connections could be formed. Connections are formed according to our objectives. There is always a logical aspect to human connections, with our objectives based on certain value system either defined individually or socially. Conversational strategies are the rhetoric that builds wider connections.

Humans have been performing this dance for centuries, in various stages of advancement. Even though we are individuals with different natures, and purposes with free will, we are somehow part of a large entity, something that keeps us connected at the elementary level. We find comfort and confidence in the knowledge that our existence is not alone but connected with others, and our lives are intricately joined to other lives. We analyze and question the human relationships, trying to define individual capacities in collective actions yet we forget that human connections are everywhere.

Human connectedness is part of the human progress. Our progress is due to our ability to form networks, and work as collectives for common solutions. We commonly build our happiness on our relationships to other people, on our bonds and ties. Even though we highly regard individual freedom, our strength is in our bonding and bridging capacities. Our connections and our engagements create cultures, and our understanding and acceptance of other cultures is a result of the understanding built through relationships. The contemporary religious environment of intolerance may partly be due to the breakdown in the connections among stakeholders. On the other hand, connectedness plays a great role in violence against humanity and intolerances, which has been an undesirable yet integral part of the society.

Connectedness is the foundation for the social cohesion. It builds social empathy because people who are connected understand, sympathize, and empathize with fellow human beings. My mother's connections to her immediate society are built on sympathy, being able to understand the need for links, even though by nature she is hesitant and reserved. Connections create togetherness, enhances the bonding, and bridging of individuals in various strata to realize and achieve common goals.

5.2 Impacts and Issues

5.2.1 Time Redefined

> The human nervous system exists in the present tense. We live in a continuous 'now'...
> Digital technologies do not exist in time, at all. By marrying our time-based bodies and
> minds to technologies that are biased against time altogether, we end up divorcing our-
> selves from the rhythms, cycles, and continuity on which we depend for coherence
> (Rushkoff 2010: 22).

In this statement, Rushkoff was trying to express the continuum of time interpreted in two different yet constantly interacting entities: the human being and
digital technology. Contemporary human being is highly associated with digital
technology, to a point where they neglect to recall the timeless quality of technology, instead absorbed themselves into the abyss of timelessness, which is against
the basic nature of humans.

As Rushkoff (2010) says, timelessness is the most attractive aspect of the connectedness. Early Internet was a slow process, with a dial through access involving
number of devices, and the service has always been expensive. Although, in ret-
rospect, this was a tedious process, the practice was premeditated, with time con-
strains. It was a shared experience all over the world, since everyone connected at
their convenience which makes the conversation on the Internet, a drawn out, as Jon
Stewart puts it as "...*passing around notes in a classroom.*"

The time constraint in the back and forth

...quality of playing a chess game by mail (Rushkoff 2010: 23)

gave the users necessary time to contemplate and compose. Since Internet pursuits
were not in real time, the expectations were of not instantaneous responses; thus,
people developed sense of well-being around the Internet. It created a level of
engagement that is collaborative, thoughtful, and considerate.

However, computers are devoid of time, instead operate from one decision to
another, whether the time between those two decisions are days or years, computers
operates on the given command. Because computers are devoid of time or the value
of time is not applicable to them, people find it a conflicting situation. Every human
action within the digital world is inexplicably associated with time, with the value
associated with time. It has positive implication since the timelessness of computers
serves our secret desire to break time, on which we unintentionally design our
activities. Thus, email served the self who has taken time to contemplate and who
made "at convenience" a preferred word.

According to Rushkoff (2010), the strength of the technology is its ability to
slow down, to break up the "now." And being recipients of that technology,
individuals are able to wield certain form of power by using interactive devices,
because interactive devices engage individuals to break the continuation thus
"deconstructing the story." The constant competition for prime time in television is

in essence a fight with the interactive technology, which provides individuals with the power to change channels or the appropriation of time.

> Our cutting and pasting, mash-ups and remixes, satires, and send-ups all originated in this ability to pause, reflect and rework (Rushkoff 2010: 28)

With the Internet speed growing faster and more available, the individual habits related to time have changed. Instead of contemplating, our Internet connection is constantly updating silently, compelling us to instant reactions, and rebuttals. There are numerous applications on our devices that is informing of us of updates, constantly keeping us on alert for another update. Whether it is preferred or not, our concentration on our devices' connection to the vast online space is psychologically affecting our everyday life. We are being compelled to multitask, praising the virtues of multitasking, yet our attention span has become short, impatient, and never fully on the subject. We glanced at everything briefly, paying partial attention, trying to cram every detail at a glance. Research suggests that transferring rapidly between cognitive gears changes the attention and focus on the tasks (Dzubak 2008).

The relentless absorption with the communication devices is affecting our relationships, everyday human connections, and our connection with our physical environment. Instead of dial-up to Internet, we are continuously online, using variety of devices, synchronizing with every device, working ourselves against a timeless technology, which absorbs our time. Our goals changed from deliberation to instantaneous, an immediacy that is penetrating our brains as keeping abreast of technology. Instead, we are perpetually drained and distressed, compelled to work against time, and make impulsive decisions and responses. This is not due to the timelessness of the technology, but our expectations of the timeless quality of technology.

The perpetual sharing of information has not necessarily empowered us or engineered us towards rational decisions and actions; instead, our engagement with information has become fleeting and hurried. We expect the information to be summarized, messages short, and answers even shorter. The virtue of short messages is celebrated like in Twitter where all messages are limited to 140 characters. Yet, our control over the way we use our devices is still dubious.

There is a choice to curtail the engagement since it is not an absolute necessity at most times. However, our nature of competitiveness will make us attempt to win the timeless status of digital world, by endeavoring to force too many tasks at one time. Our brains have the capacity to adapt to different situations (Rushkoff 2010). Thus, we adapt to the changes technology produces efficiently and effectively. In this digital age, the brain is functioning more like an information processor than information storage. Considering that information is readily available, literally at the tip of your finger, processing has become the most important task for brain. Most of our brain functions, such as finding a location or finding a friend, have been assigned to computers, which functions better than our brains. However, in that process, we have lost our ability "*to call upon certain skills*" (Rushkoff 2010: 33) and the experience that makes a task a satisfactory endeavor. Therefore, it is important to recognize the time constraints on human when interacting with digital technology, which has no sense of time. Rather than accepting the control of the devices has on our everyday through this continuous connectedness, it is necessary to understand the limits and compromise on compelling need to check our device for updates.

5.2.1.1 Time Redefined—Information Overload

Adrian is constantly mentioning his overflowing inbox, which is bursting with over thirty thousand unread emails. He is distressed and feels psychologically harassed by his overfilled inbox. He is a classic example of information overload, a casualty of time continuum, and how these two can make one feel disheartened. Each day he is attempting to manage his time to address the overloaded inbox, but he is failing due to the volume of emails accumulated, shortage of time, and new emails amassing each day.

Hurst (2007) discussed about information overload at length, attempting to explain certain challenges in overloading oneself in information, and describes how best to tackle those problems that are part of the connectivity. He specifically addresses email overload, which is still part of information exchange between people. Overloading ourselves with emails, or information in any other format, is unintentionally achieved due to our mismanagement of information. Information overload is a result of our inability to differentiate between what is important and not, and our procrastinating attitude towards tackling the information in our inbox. The result is a physical and psychological discomfort, because one is challenged to tackle the problem by the compelling psychological impact of whether some important information has been unnoticed. Some individuals' email inboxes are a perfect example of the need for task coordination, since those inboxes are filled with unread, unsorted mails, simply sitting there idling, not serving any benefit. On the one hand, this is a waste of information, even though information is readily available, and an unproductive way of handling information. This is affecting everyone, because everyone is obliged to spend time to share the same information repeatedly.

Hurst is advising to "...*letting bits go*" (2007: 21), meaning clearing away one's data, and organizing information into a coherent order that makes information constructive. It is significant to make time each day for clearing out various inboxes of their contents. It could be an unattractive task that one wants to postpone endlessly; however, digital information will become overloaded if you do not process it rapidly. Systematically going through, quickly reading and discarding, and filtering messages that are unsolicited information with the intention of avoiding further cluttering of your inbox can be an answer to this information overload. A study conducted on email overload at work informs that one of the vital management strategies is

...staying aware of the incoming information... (Dabbish and Kraut 2006: 439).

The study emphasizes on the need to keep abreast on a moment-by-moment basis to avoid overload.

A brimming inbox is demoralizing the user with feeling of overflowing (Hurst 2007). Understanding that the solution for the problem of overloaded inbox is unloading is the first step in resolving the issue. Hurst (2007) has advised on several methods to combat the information overload.

1. Make time to empty inbox(es).
2. Empty inbox(es) daily, at regular intervals or at the beginning and end of the day.
3. Take actions. Not just going through the inbox and clearing of mails, but assigning tasks and then deleting.

Some individuals keep several inboxes, such as personal, workplace related, for acquaintances, thus loading oneself with several inbox-related tasks. The best policy is making time for inboxes, whether it is one or several, and empty it as a rule.

It is important to schedule inbox time, deciding on when and how to empty information. Most individuals are happy when they clear their inbox of all mails except for ten left there for further attention. They will not realize that the incoming mails will be accumulating on top of them, making more tasks for another day. This lapse in task management will be expensive in the long run, because it will overflow the inbox, making individuals psychologically unsettled.

With the popularity of instant messaging (IM), time constraint has increased because IM demands immediate attention and responses. IM does not leave space for individuals to collect, instead induces them to respond instantaneously. This will put more pressure on overloaded inboxes because considerable amount of time will be spent on IM. This is where Hurst's "steady state" method is very important to practice (Hurst 2007). It advises on emptying inbox as a regular practice, since it can be psychologically calming. To defeat the unproductivity of overloaded inbox, it is creative to initiate a plan to unload inbox that suits each person, depending on the time availability and requirements.

5.2.2 Place Redefined

The Internet has originated from The Defense Advanced Research Projects Agency (DARPA) project to develop a communication network, which could survive a nuclear war. Thus, it is decentralized, as it has no centered place or node. Presently, the Internet is in our pockets, and it also continues to have no place. It "sucks" people from their physical place to "no place."

Digital technologies are decentralized technologies (Rushkoff 2010: 35).

They operate from unknown destinations, because they have no location. However, whichever part of the planet they are, they communicate, help you to be connected, and stay engaged. With digital technologies, we are connected globally, and our communications are expanded; thus, our focus is global, which makes us disconnect from the sense of place. The sense of place signifies our relationships within a certain measurable parameter, where we have personal, mostly face-to-face encounters and interactions. The virtue of digital media is its disengagement to a place, instead people creates places centered on it. The digital technologies' connection with people and people's disconnection with the physical place is the modern trajectory that somehow became the everyday life.

In the digital world, place represents certain realities, all associated with the digital communication. Going to places has significance as it creates a perception of the individual on their social media pages. Most contemporary travelers are going to places to be seen by their group of friends on digital world, and it is no longer the next-door neighbor, but individuals spread around the world. The objectives associated with place have moved away from local to global. The representation of place has been appropriated to represent a digital expectation of personality. Thus, the creation of place through experiences has changed with the recreation of the objectives of experience. The contemporary digital individuals understand their experiences associated with the places by attaching a digital value to them—a value which redefines the experience that creates the concept of place. A young individual sharing a photograph of her/his self on a mountain top with the full view below is rather about the reaching the top, being on the top, than sharing the experience of reaching the top. It signifies the appropriation of place in the context of communicating an idea of highest achievement, when reaching the top is an experience altogether.

The interpersonal relationship with the place has gone through a paradigm change in recent years. There was a time when big businesses have sidelined the local businesses, making their customer part of a bigger experience of shopping. That has affected the interpersonal relationships among the local merchants and their patronage. Even though the demand and supply is a competitive business, mesmerizing consumers with the persuasive power of advertising, even though individual choice and availability of options draw people to big businesses, the interpersonal relationship with the merchant round the corner plays a big role in creating a cohesive society. The solution to the small businesses trying to survive the lure of the superior shopping experience arrived from digital media: the Internet. The Internet shopping experience is lucrative for small businesses fighting for their corner from large ventures; however, the disadvantage is the loss of person-to-person contact that manifested social interactions.

Nevertheless, there are numerous occasions that digital media produce social connection that create productive outcomes, such as connecting like-minded individuals or groups, problem-centric people or activists. The communication space offered for individuals with special needs, such as incurable deceases or social phobias, helps them to exchange and cope with their pain, loss, and other issues. However, virtual interactions need to be integrated with the real life, in person interactions, where individuals interact in both manners and have the best of both worlds.

Fig. 5.1 Digital technology is not intended to alienate us away from our human encounters

…those back-and-forth exchanges are occurring at a distance. They are better than nothing - particularly for people in unique situations – but they are not a replacement for real interactions (Rushkoff 2010: 42)

Our conversations are moving from the real to the virtual, creating a chasm between two spaces and creating a discourse on the virtues of being on space that has no tangible boundaries. Timeless metabolism of the digital media has become an enormous part of our everyday, whether it is our interactions with others or goods and services. Whether we wished it or not the devices and the network are in our lives, sometimes unobtrusively in the background. The digital technology is not intended to alienate us away from our human encounters (Fig. 5.1); instead, it was supposed to enhance our real-life interactions. Our strength is in understanding the timeless quality of the digital media and employing that ability to enhance our long distance encounters, and develop the ability to maintain our everyday interactions without the digital media.

5.2.3 Self and Friends Redefined

A personal perspective by Chamari Edirisinghe

Our interactions online belong to us, yet it is out of our control the moment we put it "out there." I have participated in a forum on Facebook, which is building dialogues on issues related to social justice. Though I am a sporadic participant, I was academically interested in the theme, the dialogic interactions that are unfolding, and how the administers of the forum are directing the conversation. At one point, the conversation was about the rights of women and problematic of legalization of prostitution. When I participated in the discussion (the only woman to participate), one individual started to condemn me using derogatory remarks to some participants' displeasure. This attacking continued for some time before the administrator of the forum decided to ask me whether I feel abused by the unwarranted attack, by then is completely an assault on my personality and integrity. This incident is bringing forth the discussion on civility, accountability, and self on the digital media.

The digital activities of individuals are outside their physical zones because they interact in an intangible space that has no visible boundaries. This leads individuals towards *"depersonalized behavior"* (Rushkoff 2010) that question the various nuances of accountability. In real world, the accountability is scrutinized by various societal institutions, where one has to face the consequences of one's actions directly. The morality of accountability is contested "out there," on the real world, and even the consequences are reassessed and discussed. It is an open discussion, involving people with real identities. Although, individuals are fascinated by the choice to play with one's identity, in the real world, the perspective on identity is strongly biased.

The digital media presents not just speedy connections and audio/visual interactions, but also the options to play with one's identity. One can argue that the distance provides that option for individuals to masquerade and play with their identity. However, digital media gives a new definition to the distance. Moreover, digital media disassociate the person from the other with this misplaced notion of anonymity. Digital media offers security for your personal information and digital footprints, and in the same breath they offer various ambiguities for a person to play a fraud in the same virtual environment. This is an entrapment of self in an identity crisis. Being anonymous or having a fabricated identity on the digital world is attractive to test the limits of morality and ethics online.

The individual who was making derogatory remarks to me on online could be intentionally trying to bully me into submission so that the conversation would take a turn to his preference which is such a common action on real life slowly transferring to online. The difference is that he is one of the thousands of people on that forum, which makes him a stranger—a stranger who is abusing another stranger. The online identity has made that individual shed the moral character; instead assume an impetuous and insensitive attitude. His relationship to the social media platform is detached from his real body experience, and he is given a very desirable choice of playing with his identity. He has removed himself from his responsibility to be civil due to misplaced sense of distance. His sense of distance is misplaced because he is still himself, probably with an assumed name, and identity, and as a human being he is ethically and morally accountable for his words.

Online bullying is becoming a serious issue among young whose interactions are measured on the Internet in a manner that has little relevancy to offline interactions. However, even though anonymity is a resounding factor in online bullying, it was the offline social groups and relations who were responsible for much of the bullying (Mishna et al. 2009). Thus, it was the known social circles that turn to harassing in online, even though the study found out that online bullying to be more serious than the traditional "school yard" bullying. Another study found that the people who have been mistreated in digital world or in real world are not two separate groups (Hinduja and Patchin 2012).

Digital media is removing individuals from their sense of moral and ethical obligations to the next person. This statement is questionable, because there are individuals who are explicitly conscious of their online persona, self-regulating who they want to be online. However, representation of self on digital media is an experimentation of ethical and moral bounds of an individual, hence the dissimilar extremes in personalities. Would it help if it is demanded that individuals be themselves and ethically and morally correct on the Internet?

In the unsympathetic digital media environment, identity is a liability (Rushkoff 2010) as well as strength. It is a liability because complete strangers know your personal and loved ones' information which can be endangering; however, it is also a strength because one is not hiding behind false identities, and information that could rebound with consequences. Anonymity does not necessarily represent safety on digital media, nor does it give one a freedom to behave in a manner that is morally, ethically, and legally questionable. Anonymity is just another curtain to cover up particular aspect of self, but not all.

However, there could be occasions an individual needs to be anonymous such as an activist living in an oppressive regime. Equally, online crowd behavior could endanger the collective actions, because of identity. False identities and fake personas will question the integrity and credibility of the collective actions, making it a mob rather than activism. While keeping the private information out of the digital media, our participation and interactions should be conducted within the realm of actual identities. False identities will serve no purpose within the big picture.

Every now and then, individuals will encounter problem in separating online and offline self. Online self will feel more real than the offline self, due to the assumed courage in interactions. Where the real person struggles with interactions in real settings, in real society, the online person blossoms on the challenge of interacting with a complete stranger, sharing, and finding common grounds and thriving on the knowledge. Whether there is a moral and ethical position for human online/offline behavior is a very much discussed in the academia (Suler 2004; Nguyen et al. 2012; DeAndrea and Walther 2011). However, maintaining a strict sense of identity online is liberating and even empowering (Rushkoff 2010).

Integrity of our self-expressions in online matters. The irresponsibility on the digital world will not be treated with consideration or sympathy, because digital media is faceless individuals who are not answerable to any ethics or principles. It is often the case with oversharing on the Internet, where individuals share unwarranted amount of inappropriate information about themselves, thus endangering themselves and their closest. Our notion that, since all are on one big platform, freely connected to engage will promote the equality of action and a thought is only an assumption not an actual change. We modify our behavior on that assumption even when our real-world behavior is cautious. We are treating complete strangers on the Internet as our equals and trustworthy partners, because we made that assumption about millions of individuals trawling the Internet, which, in real life, sounds ludicrous. We do not particularly believe in equality and trustworthiness, but in our assumption, we simply do not see the other person.

The online digital media put stronger emphasis on the concept of friendship as the basis for building networks. However, there is always the question of whether friendships built on online digital media platforms really represent the concept. In the time, when communications between individuals or groups are not instantaneous, people wrote letters to pen pals: individuals in far off places. It was a soft development of mutual understanding and friendship which, in some cases, lasted throughout their lives. Today, on our social digital media platforms, our friends are from all corners of the world and from all walks of life. They show their interest in our contents, wish us for our birthdays, and chat with us occasionally on inconsequential or personal matters. These actions are sometimes the sum of friendship on online digital media. The perception of online friendship is limited to these activities. However, there are occasions the friend that you have online—with whom you are not a friend in real life—would meet face to face in real life. Thus, online friendship can move and practice in different social spaces.

Nevertheless, there is an argument on the quality of the online social relations on the context of the strength of their social ties. A study (Mesch and Talmud 2006) found that social relationship of adolescents online is a compensation for the lack of social support, and that the online relationships they developed are strong and meaningful. The study concluded social embeddedness of the ties is more important in supporting or hindering friendships, not the technology as such. This reveals that when examining the core value of the social relationships, it has not changed with the technology because individuals still build their relationship on the need to find their corner in the vast social order. Digital media technology gave them fast connectivity and range of means and methods, yet their connections is based on the principle of finding like-minded and supportive individuals.

However, it can be argued that the concept of friendship has evolved due to the changes in the perception of the act of being a friend. In the times when digital media was not attempting to define the friendship, friends were separated from acquaintances, and building a friendship took time, through trial and errors. Today, all the people on Facebook are friends, both individuals who have been close to us for a long time and individuals we just included into our circle. We use the term "friend" loosely, without further ado. We anticipate our "friends" to prefer our online contents, because that is the visual connection with that individual—the seal of approval. Our disapproval or approval of the "friend" has been conveyed through the inclusion (or exclusion) from the friend list. On the surface, these interactions appear to be superficial and horizontal without any depth of understanding or care. However, to a more or lesser degree, we build our friendships in the real world starting with these principles, until our ties to individuals are socially embedded. Thus, both our online and offline friendships are a social construction, but our digital media social relations are influenced by our perception of value of the act of being a friend.

5.2.4   Redefining Learning and Education

A personal perspective by Chamari Edirisinghe

Since we are no longer concerned about food, clothing, and shelter, even though there are many out there without them, we come to value the creativity, innovation, and education. My nephew who is barely 9 years old could not seem to understand that he needs to change out of his school uniform when he is home from school, even though his mother is strict on those rules. He will hang around in his school clothing, watching TV, needling his younger brother, and generally eating everything in the refrigerator. However, when he hears the sound of the gate opening, the signal of his mother's arrival, he will dash to the bathroom wash his face splashing some on his hair and change out of his school uniform. His mother, happily impressed, would praise him. Observing this scenario for several days, I commented on this to his mother, explaining why his strategy works all the time. He was simply finding a solution to his problem, without aggravating his mother and without having to have a change and a bath the moment he got home. He has worked within his time frame (until his mother arrives) using available resources (such as our lack of attention to his action) to maximize his enjoyment. How we arrive at solutions define how we approach the issues. It is very important for youth to imagine solutions, as it is very important for us to understand that their future is completely in the hyperconnected world, that their solution oriented thinking, among other things, will be part of their everyday.

My nephews and nieces are an integral part of this information overloaded and hyperconnected world. Their brains will process information faster than our brains because we crossed the impasse from analog to digital, but they were born to a completely digital world. Our comprehension that information overload is muting the capabilities of young minds is our lack of understanding of the information availability and still thinking at that impasse between analog and digital. Youngsters process information faster, skipping over the unwanted and unwarranted much quicker than out brains can comprehend.

Our experience of information is of libraries where information is limited, and information availability is limited. We searched for information within the scarcity and high demand; thus, our information is hard-won. This made the value we associated with information different from today's information overloaded times. Contemporary youth does not face this problem of information scarcity or competition, since they are weighted down with information from every corner and from every perspective. Their effort is on deciding on the available information in the least possible time frame and with minimum exertion.

Naturally, the question often asked is that on what do they spend their saved time on, to which I will answer later. The youths not spending much time in collecting information for their school work does not necessarily mean they do not appreciate the availability of information, or their threshold of boredom has increased, but because they find the school system still requires collecting information not voluntarily but as part of the curriculum. Therefore, it is routine for them to collect and compile information. The credibility of the information on the Internet is a long-standing conversation in the same negative tones we discussed the information overload. The information on the Internet is rapidly produced. The younger generation is aware that there is a very high amount of information available and producing more each minute, and that there is a question of trustworthiness of the information. That knowledge guides them when they are earnestly looking for trustworthy information. The information overload is not a bad omen but a richness that should be embraced, utilized, and expanded for the knowledge-building process.

I was taking a train in downtown Singapore, and I saw a group of very fashionably dressed teenagers. Most of them had two smart phones, and all of them carry tablets and headphones. It is surprising to see their fashionable bags are equipped to carry these gadgets. Like all teenagers, they giggled, joked, check their phones every 2 min, and show each other things on their tablets. And in between all these, they would endlessly text message (rather than make calls) to whoever is outside their circle. They talk, they discuss contents on their digital media pages, they text message from two different phones, using most possibly two different apps, and throughout it all from one ear they listen to music. This is the younger generation of today, communicating with both their immediate circles and outside world in this moment and this minute, while switching between devices and worlds.

This form of multitasking is the culture of youth, who transfers quickly from one task to another without a break. This is a practice that individuals from the analog to digital generation are finding unable to put into perspective. It is not because they could not comprehend the multitude of multitasking, but because they were raised to do one task at a time. Their minds are single–task-oriented—finish one and then begin another. The focus of the education is concentrating on one task at a time; however, digital generation is surpassing this one-task-oriented brain processing towards multitasking. They are processing the overflowing information by prioritizing while not letting go of the flow of information, thus switching between relevant information speedily when necessary. Their strategy is synchronously processing different types of information, possible from several devices, but when one task is prioritized, they will attend to that within that time frame and speedily switched back to the original position.

The most common criticism of multitasking is that it does not enable an individual to focus on any task properly; thus, every task is incomplete which is a question of the quality of work. The contemporary youth is constantly dealing with a large amount of information every second, and to them the value of information rests with the importance of the task. Their speed in recognizing the task and using the information to address the issues is in their ability to multitask. Their future, their professions, their recreation, etc. require processing large amount of information from numerous sources. The most important part of multitasking is the skill at recognizing and managing different attention levels and concurrently recognizes the most important task for attention without losing thread of the sequence. Those young teenagers on the train are simultaneously among their group of friends and the outside world without letting go of the flow of information from varied sources; thus, they did not miss their alighting station.

My niece, like any other kid below 10 years old, does not like school, and her teacher complains that she is distracted during the lessons. When I enquired what she thinks when she is distracted from her formal lessons, one of her reasons is that she wonders how the world holds all its species together. Apparently, the school curriculum does not include a concern like that, which forces her to curb her thirst for information, inquiry and her imagination. Thus, somewhere along the line, the formal education has failed her in facilitating her inquisitive mind, and rather than merely conforming to the situation her mind wanders imagining and processing. This is a good example of the failures in the modern education process to accommodate the contemporary mindset, where schools do not require to repeat information but to foster the imagination and facilitate its growth.

My colleague Iqmal had an experience of how the future of learning and education is shaping in Penang, Malaysia, while visiting the Penang Science Cluster,[1] which is a non-profit initiative operating in collaboration with both local governments and corporate interests. Penang has been attempting to develop the state into a knowledge hub through the development of knowledge clusters (Evers 2011). The initiative is aiming towards revitalizing the learning and education of underprivileged school children of rural areas of Penang, in collaboration with schools in those areas and volunteered instructors from industry. This is a hands-on laboratory that aims for school children to be creative and innovative. The school children learn both hardware and software, experiments in chemicals and create working prototypes out of household items, sensors and actuators. This initiative is part of their curriculum and extension of the formal learning and education system. Iqmal found out that young children are learning to code from scratch and working on embedded systems and designing drones with 3D printers.

At this point, I would like to bring back that question, On what do youngsters spend their saved time on? This is where they should most possibly use their saved time on: taking control of the information. Digital media produce information to reassemble, modify, and reproduce, and most individuals' engagement with media contents is using the existing contents. Media devices are a household item that most individuals use in everyday transactions. Most of them have considerable knowledge in using devices and existing systems which has created a divide. When the discussion on the possibilities offered by the Internet has been intense, there was a discussion on the digital divide: the have and have nots on cyberspace. Today, it is a different divide: It has become a division between the ability to control the digital contents and the dependency on the existing contents without the power to transform.

The contemporary education is required to address that concern: the ability to control the digital systems by learning to write them. That will shift the power wielded by few individuals to the common people who can write their own systems

---

[1]http://www.pscpen.com/.

using open source. The Science Cluster in Penang, Malaysia, is empowering youngsters, by enabling them to create contents and systems, and to think beyond the framework toward creativity in the hyperconnected era. The modern education, rather than building followers, should be encouraging children to take control of the existing learning and knowledge, acquiring systems to build creative minds. The young minds like my niece's ought to have her imagination and creative side uplifted and enabling them to utilize it for future.

5.2.5 Smartness and Governance

In the previous section, the discussion was on the necessity for learning and education systems to adopt techniques to prepare the future generation for the challenges of hyperconnected world. Naturally, there will be inequality in the dispersion of resources; however, it can be expected that smaller scale endeavors as social engagement projects will effectively fill the gap where policy makers fail to take actions. But these projects will not be able to change learning and education process in the long term; instead, they will provide a particular amount of support for the future innovators. For a hyperconnected future to be effective and productive requires the policy makers to think ahead, employ advisers that understand the opportunities and risks ahead, and prepare flexible policies for the future. This is especially important in developing countries that have unstable economies and political environs.

Thus, it is imperative to discuss the benefits and risks of hyperconnected technologies and smartness. Hyperconnectivity has made the world appear to be small with transnational transactions happening overnight, and our social interactions becoming global. It is not just globalization, with labor, money, information, goods and services connected intricately, but it is also shaping the everyday life of individuals living all over the world. A decision made in New York will have a profound impact on a woman living with her three children in Malawi in utter poverty, in the same manner the Malawi women impacted the decisions made elsewhere in the world. Once, when I phoned to the local airline office to change my airline reservation, my call was answered by a person in another country far away from me (using a software that most probably have been written by so many nationals, and hardware made in China) who is ready to change my flight schedule between two different continents and charge my credit card which is issued by another country. This kind of labor, money, and services cut across local and international barriers, making the whole world fall into one large system, inside which we are more connected than we would ever be able to dream of. The positive aspect is that our connectedness saves time and energy and makes us influential but at the same time we are not given a conscious choice about scope of the connectedness. Thus, hyperconnectivity is a complex process that involves many stakeholders and even affecting individuals who may perceive them as not having relation to the process.

Hyperconnectivity thus increases the risk of unintended and unplanned happening, due to the complex connections among all resources. It may appear that the local matters take precedence over the global issues to ordinary eyes. The local problems are intricately woven to the global issues, taking local to the global in an unexpected manner. When 2013–14 Thailand political crisis became increasingly uncontrollable, it is not just Thai stock market, and tourist industry that was unbalanced, but also several businesses in other countries which are depending on their outsourced products (Sethapramote 2014). The adverse impact on the tourist industry in Thailand has been profitable for other countries in the region which absorbed the influx of foreign tourists to exotic places. Thus, the political crisis in Thailand has shaken several business interests, thus delaying the production and impacting the economies and also positively impacting several other countries rich in tourism. Watching the political protest all over the world on TV, whether it is in Paris or China, it is still impacting every individuals' future, the same way the mass massacres in African countries or mass immigration crisis in Europe are impacting the whole world. It is because we are complexly connected, both real and virtual through network that covers the world from one end to another.

Goldin and Mariathasan (2014) claim that understanding the dynamics in the global system is vital to sustainable global development. This risk is not understanding the underlying forces and underestimating the probability of a safety risk. However, according to Goldin and Mariathasan (2014), the biggest risk is not the collapse of these systems, but the lack of capacity and planning to manage the complexities and interdependencies among systems. It is imperative to organize the capabilities to avoid or minimize the risk factors in hyperconnected systems, because one mismanage instance will cost substantially across the board. The concept of smart governance is very important as a practice for this particular reason to understand, estimate, and plan for risks in complexities of hyperconnectivity.

Quoting Goldin and Mariathasan, in 2009, the President of USA Barak Obama made a speech at the Cairo University presenting a framework on which the concept of smart governance can be based on, even though US is scarcely a good example of smart governance.

> When a financial system weakens in one country, prosperity is hurt everywhere. When a new flu infects one human being, all are at risk. When one nation pursues a nuclear weapon, the risk of nuclear attack rises for all nations. When violent extremists operate in one stretch of mountains, people are endangered across an ocean. And when innocents in Bosnia and Darfur are slaughtered, that is a stain on our collective conscience. That is what it means to share this world in the 21st century. That is the responsibility we have to one another as human beings.... Given our interdependence, any world order that elevates one nation or group of people over another will inevitably fail.... Our problems must be dealt with through partnership; progress must be shared (Goldin and Mariathasan 2014: 200).

The smart governing is a global requirement, because all concerns, whether it is political unrest in Middle East or estimated population rise in Asia or dubious economic practices in corporate world, are experienced globally through the hyperconnectivity. Thus, how a particular country is governed is no longer just a national concern, but a global enterprise. This idea will challenge the concept of sovereignty of a country, although smart governing will not impede on the independence of a country but will make it prepare for challenges of global order. It is existing within national parameters and transacting within a global arena. It is understanding the risk associated with hyperconnectivity within the country, the region, and globally, and building bridges, sharing information, and collectively working towards forecasting, planning, and finding solutions that is called smart governance.

With so much resources at hand, and knowing the complexity of hyperconnectivity, it is not difficult to strategize the smart governing concepts although it could be problematic if overreached. One of the problematics of overreaching is the obstructing the rights of privacy and individual freedom. When Edward Snowden defected from USA with confidential information, his revelations put a new shape to the concept of privacy and freedom. How much the safety is worth when it is up against individual freedom and right to privacy? David Brin quotes Hal Norby saying

> Sacrificing anonymity may be the next generation's price for keeping precious liberty, as prior generations paid in blood (Brin 1999)

This is a broad subject that challenges certain ethical and moral roots. In the hyperconnected world, all my interactions are online, from money transactions to intimate phone calls, and I was assured that all my information will be encrypted and will not be used by a third party; however, the government will be having a "backdoor" password as a third party to access my online footprints. After the terrorist attack in San Bernardino, California in 2015, where the attacker has used an iPhone, the US government is embroiled in a legal battle with the Apple phone company compelling them to release the encrypted access to the phone of the assailant (Khamooshi 2016). Apple has been fighting against a federal court order to secure their right not to provide a "back door" pass. Even though this issue appears to be a simple national security concern, the underlying issues are of individual privacy and security, and in particular the governmental overreach that could have different impacts in other countries.

On the other hand, I am not offered an option to excuse the hyperconnected infrastructure; thus, I am deeply embroiled in sacrificing my privacy and freedom to be connected with the world. Today, more than yester years, individuals' connections become a tool that can control their everyday actions, unknowing to them and without making them aware. Brin (1999) saw this as a "transparent society." The future challenge will be how individuals will adapt to living transparent lives, being part of a large picture that is beyond their imagination and always been monitored, measured, and analysed. Similarly, it is important to question and examine closely the measures taken by institutions of authority with information that has clear labels of "private" on them.

Hyperconnected society is sustainable when governance is transparent and accountable and continually responsive to the citizen concerns. The smartness is not merely the technological advancement, but also strategizing for unexpected. It is engaging citizenry, keeping the dialogue alive and employing rational approaches that are soft and empathetic. Individuals all over the world will be tested by the future developments in hyperconnectivity to make their voices heard above the corporate interests and corrupted authorities. They will have the advantage in being connected which is a great leap to citizen engagement, but their major task will be appointing representatives who understand the risks and concerns and who will work toward policies that are future-hyperconnectivity-oriented.

5.3 The Challenges of Future

The concept of hyperconnectivity is without any doubt is built for a better world. It is no longer a local concern but a global endeavor, and without better future for the whole world, hyperconnectivity will not be a sustainable prospect. Thus, it is still coming to the existing problems such as economic inequality, war, and global decision making, and the solutions each nation, regional powers, and global powers are arriving at. As mentioned above, every nation required to realize that their decisions are not local but "glocal" (global in approach local in concerns), which understands the challenges of being part of a hyperconnected world and adopting policies that coordinate with regional and global policies.

Even though the world is interconnected closely and each natural or man initiated act has far reaching impacts, at the bottom level not everyone is accommodated equally to be benefited from hyperconnectivity. Some countries and cities profit heavily from hyperconnectivity, the physical and virtual connectedness, while some countries, even though they experience the impact of connectedness hardly experience the benefits. Hyperconnectivity has changed the nature of the inequality, which is now associated more with the place than social class (Goldin and Mariathasan 2014). The dialogue on inequality has changed too, deviated away from Marxist ideals toward ideas on regulations on trading to fairness and managing wealth. Thus, to benefit from the hyperconnectivity, governance required to be transparent and accountable and citizens ought to change their expectations to "glocal", both local and global. To achieve this, the conversation on national level must be of global reach. The policies should reflect the inclusion of all, not favor special interest groups. According to Stiglitz (2012), the problem is the governments' unpreparedness to handle the opportunities of connectedness and their poor management of the phenomenon.

Equal opportunity for women is another matter that is important in the hyperconnected future. When Viola Davis won the Emmy award in 2015, she became the first black woman to win Outstanding Actress in a Drama award. Her acceptance speech is about being black and a woman in an industry which celebrates women as symbols (Viola Davis Wins Emmy Awards 2015). My co-author Chamari grew up in a middle-class family of four in Sri Lanka, where as a girl she was given almost the same opportunities as her brothers, to have an education and to pursue a carrier. However, it was outside of her home that she saw the gender inequality: in the school, university, and later at work. Somewhere outside her home, she was unequally treated because she is a woman. Gender inequality is not a necessity but a social construction and it is mismanaging, under-utilizing, and unfairly treating a sector of society. There are women in Afghanistan who are gang-raped, women in Sudan who gave birth to children of gang rape, and child brides in India who marry older men in ritualistic marriages. The hyperconnected world has a long way to go to liberate women from male dominance and in a hyperconnected society gender inequality will have long-term repercussions considering women are a highly valued part of the society.

Hyperconnectivity is a realization for a sustainable future. It is about harnessing the smartness, making decisions feasible, flexible, and "glocal." The increasing physical and virtual connectedness increased opportunities through information availability, and access to education is producing informed citizenry, equipped with the ability to politically engage effectively. The connectedness is producing global and local collaborations that are bringing together dynamic individuals from all corners of the globe who understand the opportunities and risks in a hyperconnected world. They have the capacity to contribute to problem solving and decisions making that will be collective in its agenda and broader in its objectives. The advantage of hyperconnectivity is the new perception, merging old and new together. Hyperconnectivity is not a curse, unless global and local entities mismanage the opportunities it offers.

References

Brin D (1999) The transparent society: will technology force us to choose between privacy and freedom? Basic Books, New York

Christakis N (2013) The science of social connections. Edge foundation inc. Accessed 01 Mar https://edge.org/panel/nicholas-christakis-the-science-of-social-connections-headcon-13-part-v

Dabbish LA, Robert EK (2006) Email overload at work: an analysis of factors associated with email strain. In: Proceedings of the 2006 20th anniversary conference on computer supported cooperative work. ACM, pp 431–440

DeAndrea DC, Joseph BW (2011) Attributions for inconsistencies between online and offline self-presentations. Commun Res 0093650210385340

Dzubak CM (2008) Multitasking: the good, the bad, and the unknown. J Assoc Tutoring Prof 1:1–12

Evers HD (2011) Knowledge cluster information as a science policy: lessons learned.

Goldin I, Mike M (2014) The butterfly defect: how globalization creates systemic risks, and what to do about it. Princeton University Press, Princeton

Hinduja S, Patchin JW (2012) Cyberbullying: neither an epidemic nor a rarity. Eur J Dev Psychol 9:539–543

Hurst M (2007) Bit literacy: productivity in the age of information and e-mail overload. Good Experience Press

Khamooshi A (2016) Breaking down Apple's iPhone fight with the U.S. Government. The New York Times

Mesch GS, Talmud I (2006) Online friendship formation, communication channels, and social closeness. Int J Internet Sci 1:29–44

Mishna F, Saini M, Solomon S (2009) Ongoing and online: children and youth's perceptions of cyber bullying. Child Youth Serv Rev 31:1222–1228

Nguyen M, Bin YS, Campbell A (2012) Comparing online and offline self-disclosure: a systematic
    review. Cyberpsychol, Behav Soc Networking 15:103–111
Rushkoff D (2010) Program or be programmed: ten commands for a digital age. Or Books,
    New York
Sethapramote Y (2014) The economic consequences of Thailand's political crisis. The Nation
Stiglitz J (2012) The price of inequality. Penguin, UK
Suler J (2004) The online disinhibition effect. CyberPsychol Behav 7:321–326
Viola Davis Wins Emmy Awards (2015) In 2015. ABCEntertainment

Chapter 6
Conclusion

Hyperconnectivity is the future for sustainable outcomes. It is connecting people, goods and services, machines, and virtually all things that can be connected. It will connect people to people, people to machines, machine to machines, and all those things collectively forming an unimaginable network of peoples and machines. In words, this may sound ambiguous and questionable however, we have discussed the different approaches to this interconnectedness of man and machine.

Our chapters discussed the various attempts at connecting people with machines and machines with machines. We have incorporated several social and cultural aspects to enhance, and added value to the man–machine connections. In one chapter, we made inroads into a controversial topic of intimacies between humans and robots, where we attempt a logical discussion on love and sex between humans and robots. We also introduce how multisensory ambiances can be embedded into systems to digitally reproduce human's five sensations and the future possibilities those experiments offer. All those researches encompass the hyperconnected future we are featuring here.

Hyperconnectivity has the ability to build connections that are collective in its approach. As we have been deliberating throughout this book, connections are not new to human beings. Our progress is due to us constantly seeking new connections, building bridges, and creating networks. Our historical milestones are all related to our need to communicate and to our need for connections. Those are not mere connections, but meaningful ones that add value to lives. Hyperconnectivity will expand on those connections, bringing together different stakeholders, such as man–machine, machine–machine, and machine–man–machine collective collaborations. These collectives will shape the future communications and connectedness.

Hyperconnectivity is frequently either misunderstood on moral grounds or over amplified to a proportion that is unrealistic. Popular media contributed to these extreme views by creating narratives that are futuristic, but emphasizing the supposed negative aspects. In practice, hyperconnectivity is simply a connectivity that

© The Author(s) 2016

A.D. Cheok, *Hyperconnectivity*, SpringerBriefs in Human–Computer Interaction, DOI 10.1007/978-1-4471-7311-3_6 is going beyond the conventional connections, involving machines, people, and things. These connections will redefine certain facets of everyday life, such as time, our everyday relationships, and our perception of self. It will change our everyday interactions with people, machines, and things. It will change our daily practices, such as our work which will be efficient, less time spent at an office, and our leisure will be equally redefined, with so much of it spend on hyperconnected environments. Our financial transactions will be simpler, less time-consuming, and conducted using a mobile device. Our logistics of our travel and transportation is complex yet simpler at the other end, because the services are connected and interconnected. Our cities are efficient and productive, providing citizens with robust options of living. Hyperconnectivity will maximize the cities to be dynamic, experimenting with the availability of data, accommodating data for better service and perceptions. Hyperconnectivity will transform the system of education, because connectivity will compel the formal system to include certain informalities that will facilitate the future of learning. Our political engagement will be active on a different plain, unlike in Tahrir Square[1] where people came in masses to change a political regime with little impact on the political system, influencing the political structure and compelling the governments to become smart and good in governing approaches.

All these transformations will herald a new future, where connectivity plays a silent role of major proportions. As we have been discussing throughout this book, the need to connect has driven us through centuries, and not just intangibly but also various ways of connecting tangibly. Our need for easy transfer of money and information made us think of different ways to connect, thus saving time and efforts. Our need to explore, experiment with our capabilities to connect, and expand connections has been the driving force in arriving at hyperconnectivity. Thus, it is time to recognize the opportunities offered by a hyperconnected world and try to expand toward an inclusive global extent.

---

[1]http://www.huffingtonpost.com/news/tahrir-square-protests/
http://www.theguardian.com/world/2011/feb/01/ahdaf-soueif-egypt-protests.

Epilogue

To end this book on hyperconnectivity, we would like to present a short story written by the futurist **Hernán Ortiz**, *who visualizes the life in a hyperconnected future.*

The Lost Art of Taking Time Off

I found the best coffee in the world while flying to the city of Cartagena. It popped-up on page # 7 of the travel magazine tucked into the rear seat pocket. My taste piercing unveiled a rich flavor with medium acidity and notes of chocolate and ripe fruits. My olfactory piercing wafted out a nutty-caramel aroma. The ad managed to shook me out of the discomfort of being sandwiched between two overweight executives, and just for one moment, I had a sense of inner peace.

When you get used to multisensory advertising (the coconut-scented beaches, the vanilla-smelling cars, the champagne-fragranced jewelery) you just want to leave them behind by turning pages until you reach the juicy content. Only skilfully designed advertising claims to have accomplished the amazing feat of capturing people's attention. With the certification of authentic in-person experience—the kind you could n't translate to a multisensory digital format—Café Castillo, located in the walled city, promised to be one of the remaining places in the world that are worth traveling to.

As part of my job in the multisensory marketing industry, I've grown skeptical of such statements. If it were not for my psychbot, who squared away everything related to my vacation (restricting access to my inbox and IMs, picking up the destination, booking the tickets and hotel), I wouldn't be so keen on visiting an in-person coffee shop. I would have allowed my budgetbot to turn on my own coffeemaker, but I doubt he would have shown up. My psychbot often blocks him out of the system, given priority to my happiness instead of wealth accumulation. Again and again, my psychbot has proven that her decisions are more sensible than mine. Increasing her monthly budget (which is why she was able to buy the tickets without consulting me) has had a noteworthy effect on my mood, something that can be verified by the decreased blood cortisol levels found in my medical record.

© The Author(s) 2016

A.D. Cheok, *Hyperconnectivity*, SpringerBriefs in Human–Computer Interaction, DOI 10.1007/978-1-4471-7311-3

My psychbot also increased the frequency of the samples my gloves sensors send to analyze the chemicals in my sweat.

One of the best decisions taken by my psychbot was purchasing a clonebot, a simulation that smells like me, moves like me, and thinks almost like me, thanks to the computer modeling of my behavioral patterns. According to my psychbot, the relationship I had with my mother was directly related to my emotional issues. My mom expected at least five minutes of remote interaction. Five minutes. That might be the difference between having or not having a job. My mom did not understand the challenges of living in a hyperconnected 24/7 availability world.

Clonebot was programmed to establish a connection with my mom every other day, greet her with a warm hug, and listen to her monologue of health issues. The simulation, through generic conversation, made my mom thinks that she was talking with me when in reality she was talking to a digital copy of me. Clonebot simulated liking the food she cooked by telling her it was delicious in multiple, software-generated ways. He even asked sometimes for the 3D food printer recipe to pretend to have it for dinner. It was a win–win situation because after my psychbot talked with my mom's doctorbot she found out her cortisol levels were back to normal.

Finding sexual partners is one of the few activities I decided to invest my time on. I had refined the search algorithm of my wingbot to only find women who are as busy as me, with no emotional attachments and sexually liberated. The interface highlighted a woman sitting four rows ahead of me. I swirled my index finger to look at every angle of her 3D representation. She was definitely in the attractive range, calculated by my wingbot based on pupil dilation, heart rate variability, and breathing patterns. While I was checking her out, I accessed the options that were available only to users who matched her attractiveness settings, including personality traits and sensory information: body odor, skin texture, and kissing style. I took my Kissenger device out of my carry-on bag and selected the last option, by staring and blinking at it. Right next to me, one of the obese executives was kissing her lover good-bye, so I activated the "customize environment" option to conceal my fellow passengers and focused on my possible sexual partner. The seats looked empty, as if I were alone in the plane. I joined my lips with the Kissenger's silicone lips, but instead of the slow, sizzling kiss I was expecting from her, I felt her slurpy tongue flopping around my mouth like an out-of-water fish. I removed the Kissenger, stared at wingbot's exit button, and clicked with a blink. "Do you want to add this kissing style to the list of unwanted features?" asked my wingbot before shutting down. I clicked yes with a blink.

Disappointed, I looked down to the magazine on my lap. Once again, the marvelous flavor took over my tongue and nose. A Chemex coffeemaker popped-up the page, a visualization of the entire stock of the origin that was being advertised, its content accurately decreasing every time someone took a sip from their cup at the coffee shop. You could see their profile images submerged in the black liquid like stubborn bubbles, and if you stare at them, you could read their reviews on social networks. I didn't want to be biased by their opinions, so I just stared at the ad's sharing button, clicked with a blink and sent it to my co-workers, who were finishing their daily stand-up meeting. I wanted to see their reaction, so I decided to join the call and entered the conference room.

"Aren't you on vacation?" my boss said.

"Yes, I'm going offline soon, just wanted to share this with you really quick." At the center of the table, the Café Castillo ad popped-up. My co-workers smelled and tasted the coffee and gave themselves time to process the experience.

"It's a masterpiece!" my boss said, mesmerized by the Chemex coffeemaker, the real-time visualization, the bubble-clients. "I've never experienced such an engaging advertising."

"Me neither. I'll go in person to understand how they managed to simulate the flavor," I said, right before my psychbot disconnected the call.

"You'll go for a cup of coffee and that's it," my psychbot said, using her higher access level to intrude without my authorization. "You're such a workaholic! It's been six years since your last vacation."

"Help me, then," I said. "Teach me the lost art of taking time off."

"That's easy," she said. "Just focus on anything other than marketing. Why don't you feed Truffle?"

I had already automated the feeding process, but my psychbot set up a connection with the holoprojector to interact with my dog. When the connection was made, a bell alerted Truffle. She went running and wagging her tail until she placed her front paws on my holo's chest. I felt the weight of her paws in my jacket and she found support in the holo's magnetic interface. Through my gloves I felt the fur in her back while I petted her. After the excited greeting, Truffle sat down to wait for her food. I stared at the feeding option, clicked with a blink and the holoprojector's hatch opened. A bowl of dog food was pushed out by the magnetic interface. Truffle ate the bowl clean before it was pulled back inside.

The magnetic interface tossed a ball, following the direction and strength I indicated with my gloves, and Truffle caught it, brought it back to my holo, and dropped it on the floor to play again. Our fetch game got interrupted by a high-priority landing notification sent by the plane. Before getting off, I stared at the coffee ad's "directions" button and clicked with a blink.

A driverless cab waited for me at the airport to take me to the Movich hotel, located in the walled city. I dropped the bags and walked through narrow streets, following the blue line guiding me toward Café Castillo. I walked past striking colonial houses with flower-decorated balconies, many of them transformed into commercial properties. Given my unusual location, my touristbot came up with restaurant recommendations, touristic attractions and beach reviews by social media friends. ID tags all over Santo Domingo plaza helped me learn more about the place: the sixteenth century church at the center, the Fernando Botero statue Gertrudis (whose ass you're supposed to touch for good luck, or so my boss said in a geonote), and the long-awaited Café Castillo.

The outdoor seating option reminded me of famous European cafés. While waiting in line, I made my order through the interface, paid with bitcoins and a barista looked over my head to read the order. I imagine she was looking at a 3D Chemex animation with a huge number on top indicating how many cups I requested. The barista served the order on a cup that had been previously used by 35 people, none of them in my social network. The cup asked me if I wanted to check in. I stared at the yes option, clicked with a blink and sat outside. If my boss was still looking at the advertising, he may have noticed my disgusted face in one of the bubbles. He may have concluded that the experience did not match the one they promised me. It was just another company that had invested a large amount of money in a multisensory design that did not represent the reality of the product. While my taste piercing sweetened the burnt, ashy, sour notes, I thought we were living in a strange world where in-person experiences were surpassed by the digital. That gloomy realization brought me down to a daunting state that was interrupted by my psychbot.

"You're thinking about marketing again," she said. "Here's what you have to do: inhale the salty Caribbean air, run into the ocean fully clothed, drink a cocktail in the pool. Have authentic experiences, things you only do on vacation."

My psychbot was right, as always, but she had forgotten something on her list. I accessed the menu and killed active processes, one by one, including my clonebot.

I called my mom. When was the last time I heard her voice? I didn't recognize that senile tremor. And her face… Jesus, why was her face so dry? Why did she have so many wrinkles?

I felt the flaccid arms of an old lady through my jacket, a stranger who had stopped smiling because she was unsure if I was really her son. I listened to her monologue about her health while sipping disguised coffee. She was brief this time: Her doctorbot gave her an estimate. She shared the taste and recipe of the soup she was cooking. I tried to make conversation about it, but the estimate was swirling around my head. I couldn't stand to be there. I hugged her good-bye and tried to activate my clonebot, but I couldn't. My psychbot had already removed it from the system.

Index

Printed in the United States
By Bookmasters